IF I KNEW THEN
WHAT I KNOW NOW

IF I KNEW THEN
WHAT I KNOW NOW

CEOs and Other

Smart Executives

Share Wisdom

They Wish They'd

Been Told 25 Years Ago

RICHARD EDLER

B
BERKLEY BOOKS, NEW YORK

IF I KNEW THEN WHAT I KNOW NOW

A Berkley Book / published by arrangement with
the author

PRINTING HISTORY
G. P. Putnam's Sons edition / January 1996
Berkley trade paperback edition / January 1997

The Putnam Berkley World Wide Web site address is http://www.berkley.com/berkley

ISBN: 0-425-15609-5

BERKLEY®
Berkley Books are published by The Berkley Publishing Group,
200 Madison Avenue, New York, New York 10016.
BERKLEY and the "B" design
are trademarks belonging to Berkley Publishing Corporation.

Printed in the United States of America

1   3   5   7   9   10   8   6   4   2

ACKNOWLEDGMENTS

To my wife, Kitty, and my son, Rick, who gave me the love, support, and encouragement to write this book and fulfill my dream. No one can give another person a greater gift.

I thank Greg Shapiro, Lyn Teven, Stacy Creamer, and Eric Simonoff, who championed this book from the beginning and helped edit it with tough love.

This also acknowledges two organizations who have been a special part of my life and this book: the Young Presidents' Organization and the American Association of Advertising Agencies.

Most important, I thank the contributors themselves who make up this collection. They volunteered their most candid hindsights and wisdom for only one reason—to try to give back a little from their own experience in business and life so others could get a jump start.

This book is dedicated to the memory of
Mark Merryweather Edler
1973–1992

INTRODUCTION

This book is a collection of different people's responses to the same question: "What do you know now that you wish you'd been told twenty-five years ago?"

The collection really started twelve years ago. I was president of an advertising agency in Los Angeles and was invited to speak at a business commencement at California State University in Bakersfield. The honor of the invitation caused me to say yes. But the responsibility caused me to pause and ask myself what I could possibly offer that would have "take home" value to young graduates just starting out. The answer was very little.

By myself I simply did not have the life experience to pontificate from a podium to a bunch of students. But I did have something unique—a job that gave me remarkable access to presidents and CEOs of many different companies. So to prepare my talk, I asked ten clients this same hindsight question. The answers were fun and made up the mosaic of what became a nice speech.

Since then this little "collection" has mushroomed. Sometimes one person's hindsight conflicts with another's. Some thoughts are heavy. Some are light. A few are "anonymous" at the request of the contributor. Many are from the advertising field because that is my background.

What all contributors have in common are two things: (1) they have "made it" to the top of their fields, and (2) they care enough to very candidly share their hindsight in order to help "mentor" someone else. I can't imagine a nicer way to give back.

The responses appear randomly, like a smörgasbord buffet. Select whatever will help you. In some cases, I have added my own thoughts and commentary, which appear inside the vertical bar on each page.

My wish for you is that you can know now what others wish they knew back then—but learned the hard way—so you don't have to.

—Richard Edler
April 1995

What a man knows at fifty that he did not know at twenty is, for the most part, incommunicable . . . all the observations about life which can be communicated handily are as well known to a man at twenty who has been attentive as to a man at fifty. He has been told them all, he has read them all, but he has not lived them all.

What he knows at fifty that he did not know at twenty is not the knowledge of formulas or forms of words, but of people, places, actions—a knowledge gained by touch, sight, sound, victories, failures, sleeplessness, devotion, love—the human experiences and emotions of this earth and of oneself and of other men; and perhaps, too, a little faith, and a little reverence for things you cannot see.

—ADLAI E. STEVENSON

From a speech to the senior class at Princeton University, 1954.

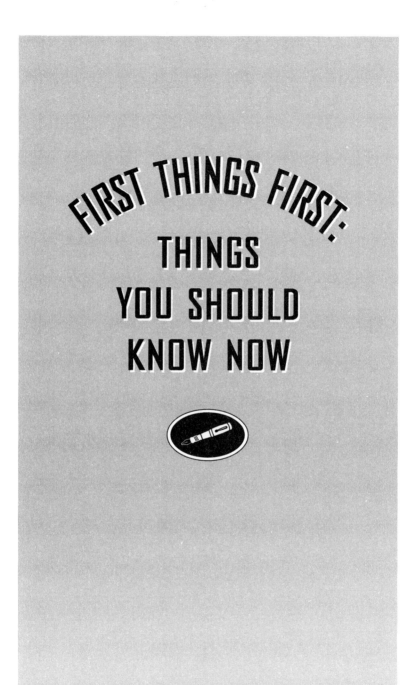

FIRST THINGS FIRST:
THINGS
YOU SHOULD
KNOW NOW

First Things
First: Things
You Should
Know Now

You are 100 percent responsible for your own happiness. Other people aren't responsible. Your parents aren't responsible. Your spouse isn't. You alone are. So if you are not happy, it's up to you to change something. It's not up to someone else to "fix it" for you.

—DR. GERALD D. BELL
PROFESSOR, KENAN-FLAGLER
GRADUATE SCHOOL OF BUSINESS
UNIVERSITY OF NORTH CAROLINA

This is my favorite definition of a goal. What are your dreams and goals? To find out, try these simple thought starters:

1. Make a list. What would you do if you had only six months to live? If you never had to worry about money again? This is the real you.

2. Draw an ideal picture of yourself in five years. Where are you and what are you doing? With whom?

3. Imagine your own funeral some day. Three people rise to give eulogies about you—one from your family, one from business, and one from the community. Who are they? What would they say about your life? What would you *want* them to say?

The differences between these things and where you are today help frame your goals.

Have a goal. A goal is just a dream with a deadline.

—MARJORIE BLANCHARD
AUTHOR

When in doubt, do it.

In my professional career as well as my personal investments, trying new things has paid off more than 90 percent of the time. I'm glad I did it, and I wouldn't want it any other way.

Even the 10 percent of experiences that can be unpleasant help you appreciate the other 90 percent all the more.

—DAVE CHRISTENSEN
PARTNER, ERNST & YOUNG

First Things First: Things You Should Know Now

In your twenties, you have time. Experiment. Explore. Don't make decisions quickly. In your twenties, you find what you like and what you don't like.

Then, sometime in your thirties, you find your career.

Come your forties, you build your career.

And in your fifties, you enjoy your career.

We all need to relax more. We need perspective to evaluate our own achievements. The measurement process is better left to decades.

—COCHRANE CHASE
FORMER CHAIRMAN,
COCHRANE CHASE LIVINGSTON

1. Do what is right. If you aren't sure, ask yourself this question: "How will my actions, taken in private, look if published on the front page of the newspaper my mother and father read?" You never need to lie or cheat to succeed in life.

2. Make a "secret" list of things you want to do before you check out. Put it in your billfold or purse and look at it from time to time. Examples might include a balloon ride, a river raft down the Colorado, catching a five-pound bass, visiting the Taj Mahal, climbing the Great Wall, or snow skiing. Don't forget the little pleasures—a sunset, a walk along the beach, cold beer, or a kiss behind the ear. Develop a broad range of experiences. Don't define yourself solely by your job.

—TOM JOHNSON
PRESIDENT, CABLE NEWS NETWORK

First Things First: Things You Should Know Now

First Things First: Things You Should Know Now

You come to work every day to solve problems. If snafus, glitches, personality conflicts, and Murphy's Law drive you crazy, don't go into business.

Solving problems is purposeful and satisfying for those of us who love business. Welcome them.

—PLEASANT ROWLAND
PRESIDENT AND CHIEF EXECUTIVE
OFFICER, PLEASANT COMPANY

$$unhappiness = image - reality.$$

—DENNIS PRAGER
RADIO AND TELEVISION HOST,
RELIGION SCHOLAR, AUTHOR AND
LECTURER

Essentially, Dennis feels we are unhappy when we have an image for ourselves that we can't possibly live up to—for example, a perfect marriage and financial independence by age forty. This image is a difficult match with most people's reality. So there is an unhappiness gap $(i - r)$ between where we see ourselves and where we really are.

In Dennis's equation, you can do only two things—modify your image or your reality. The best way is to modify your image. This means recognizing how fortunate we are instead of focusing on what we don't have. Dennis believes that the ultimate key to happiness is not money or power or friends or health. The ultimate key is *gratitude*. Envy ruins happiness. Gratitude ensures it.

Show up and keep showing up. One day you look up and you are in front of the line.

—TOM COLEMAN
PRESIDENT & CHIEF
EXECUTIVE OFFICER
COLEMAN HOMES

First
Things
First:
Things
You
Should
Know
Now

The single most important thing I've learned is that you can't force things—situations or people.

When I started work, Kennedy-style activism was the way to lead; you had to identify a problem before others even knew it existed, make a plan, and solve it—even if you had to ram your solution through a staff that didn't share your sense of urgency.

Then one day, I left on a trip before I could clear out my in-basket. When I got back to the office ten days later, I discovered that 90 percent of the problems I'd left behind had solved themselves in my absence.

Insight dawned: All sorts of nettlesome policy and personnel questions have to marinate awhile before the right course of action comes clear. And when the solu-

First Things First: Things You Should Know Now

tion does appear, people more readily recognize it and accept it. Indeed, more often than not, they suggest the solution before the leader has to impose it. And they don't feel coerced.

Nearly all the missteps I've made over the years editing *Newsweek, New York* magazine, and now *Esquire* came because I convinced myself that I had to act precipitously or decisively when, in fact, there was plenty of time—if only an extra half hour on deadline—to tease the right action out of the confusion and anxiety of the moment.

—EDWARD KOSNER
EDITOR IN CHIEF,
ESQUIRE MAGAZINE

Stand for something.

—Li Lu
STUDENT LEADER,
TIANANMEN SQUARE

One day in the office of the chairman of our company, I noticed a picture of his college Board of Directors. In the center was an elderly man badly hunched over.

My chairman explained that this man was the president. When he was a young man, he played the piano professionally with great love. Then he suffered an accident which broke his back. The doctors gave him a choice. He could have his back set permanently straight like everybody else, but he would never again play the piano. Or, he could have his back set hunched over, allowing him to play but never again stand up.

He chose the piano. I'm not sure I would have, but I deeply admire his commitment to something.

Twenty-five years ago I wish someone had told me that while work is very important, the most important things involve family and friends.

Many times I chose business-related activities and trips that mean so little now, when compared to soccer games, dinners with friends, and school-night open houses that cannot be recaptured.

Then one day I lost my job after nineteen years—for no reason except the desire to cut a budget. So make time for your family and friends, take time to exercise, laugh more, and talk to people outside your company.

—CHARLES SCHMUCK
PUBLISHER, PERFORMING ARTS
MAGAZINE

I f you don't take care of your body, where will you live?

—PEGGY AYALA
REGISTERED NURSE,
CAMINO HEALTH CENTER

All our lives we hear "eat right and get exercise." We all know what to do. More than 65 percent of people in the United States say they are "on a diet" or "watching their weight." It's just hard to make it a priority. But it is worth it. As an old ad says, "When you have your health, you have everything." And when you are sick, you feel like doing nothing else but getting well again.

Good physical condition helps you think more clearly and function better all day. The benefits of fitness—health, work efficiency, attractiveness to the opposite sex, a positive self-image—are self-evident.

Make it a priority.

First Things First: Things You Should Know Now

When your children are born, and every year thereafter, write them a letter on their birthday. Save them up, but don't tell anyone. Then give your children their letters on their twenty-first birthdays.

—Rich Gold
President, R. N.
Gold & Company

You can't out-earn compound interest.

If you start saving a fixed amount at age 20 and your twin brother saves the same amount beginning at age 30, by the time you are both 65 you will have twice as much money as he does. The same is true for loving and investing in your children. It's never too soon to start.

—LARRY HIGBY
PRESIDENT, UNOCAL CORPORATION
76 PRODUCTS COMPANY

First
Things
First:
Things
You
Should
Know
Now

First Things First: Things You Should Know Now

There are three hindsights I suggest to my children—the importance of focus, tenacity, and niche selection.

Focus on the work at hand. We seem to be a society that lacks discipline and concentration.

Stick with it and be prepared to be knocked down. Believe it or not everybody gets knocked down. The most glamorous jobs in the world are not always fun and games.

Select your niche. It is very difficult to succeed in a crowded field. I have found that you can move more rapidly if you select a segment of that crowded field and become an expert in it. For example, the field of law is very crowded. A new attorney entering as a general business attorney will find slow growth. But a new attorney selecting a niche such as sports law will have the opportunity for rapid growth.

Search out that special growth segment in your field and become an expert. You will grow more quickly than you can imagine.

—JOE POTOCKI
PRESIDENT, JOSEPH E.
POTOCKI & ASSOCIATES

First Things First: Things You Should Know Now

Follow your heartbeat.

—PETER UEBERROTH
CHAIRMAN, 1984 L.A. OLYMPICS
FORMER BASEBALL COMMISSIONER

In his 1991 commencement address at the University of Southern California, Peter told the graduates "Follow your heartbeat." If you follow what you love, then all other good things, including money, will usually follow. To focus on the result—i.e., making a lot of money—is backwards.

Many people ask me to help them figure out what they should do with their lives. In fact, the most frequent response to the question this book is based on—"What do you wish someone told you twenty-five years ago?"—has been simply, "I wish someone had told me to just follow my dream."

LAST THINGS SECOND:

THINGS IT TOOK YEARS OF
EXPERIENCE TO FIGURE
OUT BECAUSE THEY DON'T
SEEM LOGICAL THOUGH
THEY ACTUALLY DO MAKE
A LOT OF SENSE

Last Things Second:
Things It Took Years
of Experience to
Figure Out Because
They Don't Seem
Logical Though
They Actually Do
Make A Lot of Sense

Always see people in their office, not yours.

When somebody asks, "Can I see you?" you say, "Sure, I'll be right over."

There are two benefits: (1) you get out from behind your desk and walk the office halls, and (2) you can always leave when you want to. You are seen by others—always good for morale—and you usually learn at least one new thing every time around the office floor.

—DICK SCHLOSBERG
PUBLISHER AND CHIEF EXECUTIVE
OFFICER, THE LOS ANGELES TIMES

Open your mail at 4:30 in the afternoon.

—CHARLIE FERGUSON
FORMER ADVERTISING MANAGER,
PROCTER & GAMBLE COMPANY

By holding your mail until 4:30, you come in each morning and have the day you planned to have. You accomplish the important things you set out for today instead of letting the mail or the latest phone call run your day for you. Then, at 4:30, after you have accomplished what you determined was important, open your mail and use it to help plan the day you are going to have tomorrow.

Humor, confidence, and a positive attitude outrank brains, connections, and experience in determining who gets ahead and who stays ahead (although the last three count, too.)

—SALLY KOSLOW
EDITOR IN CHIEF,
MCCALL'S MAGAZINE

Make lots of mistakes.

Mistakes are the fuel for fast career development. Learn how to make brilliant recoveries. And then never make the same mistake twice. Do this and your career will move faster toward the top than your more conservative associates'.

—J. MELVIN MUSE
CHAIRMAN AND CHIEF
EXECUTIVE OFFICER,
MUSE CORDERO CHEN

Do the important, not the
urgent.

In 1972 an airliner crashed on
takeoff in Florida. According to
some reports, the flight
recorder later showed that both
the pilot and co-pilot were
tinkering with a malfunctioning
indicator light and literally flew
the plane into the ground. They
were doing something that
might have been urgent, but not
important.

There is an old pilot's saying
that goes "Fly the airplane first."
Devote your time to the important. Delegate the rest.

Last Things Second: Things It Took Years of Experience to Figure Out Because They Don't Seem Logical Though They Actually Do Make A Lot of Sense

Don't listen to your mother.

Mom always told me, when expressing my point of view, to precede my words with "I think" rather than "I know." In this way, she said, I would never be embarrassed by being proven wrong. It sounded like reasonable advice then for a well-mannered young lady such as myself. She neglected to tell me that although I would never be proven wrong, I would not be seen as particularly right, either.

What I learned is that in business, corporate leaders want to surround themselves with people who "know," not those who hesitate. In my early career, I was passed over for a promotion because I seemed timid in my leadership compared to other brazen "knowers." I really did know, but had trained myself not to act that way. It took a constant cognitive effort to retrain myself to believe in my own thought process. I did "know" and most of the time what I "knew" was right.

Ultimately, my career progressed, but I lost many valuable years and even a marriage partly due to earlier insecurities. So don't let Mom or any other adult pass along their feelings or words of insecurity to you. PS. I still love my mom.

—Rita Rao
Former Executive Vice-President, Mattel Toys

Last Things Second: Things It Took Years of Experience to Figure Out Because They Don't Seem Logical Though They Actually Do Make A Lot of Sense

This may not be the way the world should be, but it is the way it often is. People look to you for signals of your competence long before you have a chance to demonstrate it.

So walk with a spring in your step, and enter a room with a smile and an attitude of quiet command. Before you speak to a group, quietly pump yourself up before going "on stage." And if you want to succeed in business, learn to speak publicly. There is something about words said from a podium that adds a majesty impossible in general conversation.

Of course, you have to back it all up with real competence. But first impressions do count a lot. If you make a bad one, you just have that much further to travel. Someone once said, "It's not who you know that counts, it's who other people think you know."

T he appearance of competence is almost as important as competence itself.

—CHUCK LIEPPE
CHIEF EXECUTIVE OFFICER,
BEROL CORPORATION

Don't worry about getting fired. If the situation really warrants it, tell your boss to go to hell.

You may get fired, but the severance will be better. Often what actually happens is that you get new respect and people regard you with more deference. More important, your stress level goes down and it's more fun to look in the mirror.

In my own case, and dozens of others I've observed, really good people always end up doing better when they get fired.

Don't bottle up your anger, angst, and frustration. Just say "Kiss my ass," and see what happens. The sheer joy and release is worth the dislocation, which really does *not* happen 90 percent of the time.

Last Things Second: Things It Took Years of Experience to Figure Out Because They Don't Seem Logical Though They Actually Do Make A Lot of Sense

Of course, it is prudent to pick your shots carefully.

—JIM FRAWLEY
PRESIDENT, FRAWLEY &
ASSOCIATES

Guess what . . . you *did* go to college to wait tables.

Do anything to get a foot in the door. I did. Others I know who made it in the entertainment business did. So take that grunt job. Be flexible. You don't know everything yet.

I worry a lot about the next generation—the people I interview in my office who want to get into the business. There is a lack of ambition and willingness to learn the business. I hear things like "I don't want to work from eight to eight every day because I won't have time for my own artistic endeavors."

You may have taken film courses in college so you have a sense of the history of the business, but you don't "know" the business until you are in it. To get in it, do anything, even if it means waiting on tables.

—KATHY JONES
EXECUTIVE VICE-PRESIDENT,
MARKETING, UNIVERSAL STUDIOS

Always take the job working on the product or the office in trouble. Never take over a business doing well.

—Tom O'Sullivan
President, Weller & O'Sullivan

This is simple common sense. If you take over a healthy growing business, the best you can do is keep it on course. However, if you take over a sick brand, for example as the new brand manager, chances are you can turn it around and be a hero. Even if you don't succeed, you have a fallback position—you did your best with problems "beyond your control."

Also, when you take over a business in trouble, luck is on your side. Many people who got credit for "turning a company around" may have no idea why the business returned to health. Often it was for reasons such as the economy or a change in competition that had nothing to do with the person in charge.

It's okay to fire your customers.

—THE WALL STREET JOURNAL

This is from an editorial that impressed me in March 1992. The *Journal* put a unique twist on good business relationships. In the advertising business there is probably nothing you can do to build morale faster in an agency than to resign a client—even when the employees know it might mean hard times and even layoffs. You see, it always goes the other way. The trade press each week headlines the firing of this or that agency by a client, and the inevitable announcement of a new agency review. Agencies always seem the spineless victim of client whims.

After a while, you start to think this is the way things are supposed to be. But truly great agencies—or any great company serving customers— have their own standards too. And there ought to be

Last Things Second: Things It Took Years of Experience to Figure Out Because They Don't Seem Logical Though They Actually Do Make A Lot of Sense

customers you really don't want and wouldn't take, regardless of revenue. Your employees need to know that abusive behavior will not be tolerated by any customer, no matter how important that customer is. That way you and your employees can truly love the customers you have—because you have mutually selected each other. It just changes how you think about everything. And it raises everyone's head up a notch in the process.

Last
Things
Second:
Things
It Took
Years of
Experience
to
Figure
Out
Because
They
Don't
Seem
Logical
Though
They
Actually
Do Make
A Lot of
Sense

Don't be afraid to start a career without knowing exactly what you want to do. Very few people do.

Then take initiative with your career and make things happen rather than waiting around for something to happen.

I interview people every day who behave as though their education or current position qualifies them for consideration for a new job. Interest, enthusiasm, and a little homework can be much more valuable.

—PETER KELLY
MANAGING PARTNER,
R. ROLLO ASSOCIATES

Don't think you have to win. What's important is getting what you want.

—Phyllis E. Grann
Chairman & Chief Executive
Officer, The Putnam Berkley
Group, Inc.

Last Things Second: Things It Took Years of Experience to Figure Out Because They Don't Seem Logical Though They Actually Do Make A Lot of Sense

THINGS YOU'LL BE BETTER OFF KNOWING

Things
You'll Be
Better
Off
Knowing

The secret to business success is doing enough of the right things in order to stay alive long enough in order to get lucky. There are three secrets to getting lucky:

1. Deal with good people. It is better to be in a bad deal with good people, than the reverse.

2. Manage costs, not revenue. And remember that there is no such thing as a fixed cost.

3. Get out at the right time. Sell a business when it has no place to go but up. That's when people will pay you the highest value on future earnings, and if they're right—God bless. This is true win-win.

—JERRY E. GOLDRESS
PRESIDENT, WHEREHOUSE
ENTERTAINMENT. CHAIRMAN,
GRISANTI, GALEF &
GOLDRESS, INC.

Buy one-third as much, three times as good.

Pay for quality and buy less. Buy and wear only good clothes. You'll look better, feel better, and have an easier time picking out your wardrobe in the morning. This doesn't just apply to clothes, but to everything in your life.

And when in doubt, throw it out. Get rid of junk. Cut your closet, your office files, and your personal baggage by two-thirds. Travel lightly through life, not burdened like a turtle.

—NITA M. ALLEN
PRESIDENT, MEADWAY
PRODUCTIONS, INC.

Work hard; take advantage of and enjoy life's many opportunities; give back.

—ORRIN HATCH
U.S. SENATOR

Never burn your bridges. Don't even spray graffiti on them.

You never know when the boss you resign from today may be hiring you again at another company, promoting you to another job in the same company, or acting as a future reference. So when you exit, always do so with grace and appreciation.

Also, always follow up with a letter to anyone who takes the time to help you get a job, leave a job, or anything in between. A written follow-up of some kind—E-Mail, telegram, fax, whatever—never goes out of style. No exceptions.

—TONY HOYT
FORMER VICE-PRESIDENT,
THE HEARST CORPORATION

Things
You'll Be
Better Off
Knowing

To decide anything, first write down the pros and cons, and then photocopy your list. Then throw the original away and look at only the copy. Also type it instead of using your own handwriting.

It is always easier to make a detached, unemotional decision by stepping back and looking at a black-and-white piece of paper. Also, don't show your pro-and-con list to someone else, or you won't be honest with yourself when you write it down.

—DENNIS POPE
FORMER CHIEF FINANCIAL
OFFICER, WEINTRAUB
ENTERTAINMENT

Things You'll Be Better Off Knowing

When I was younger plenty of people told me, but I wish someone had *convinced* me, of the significance of setting well-thought-out and meaningful goals earlier in my life, and then sticking with them.

My career would have been more rewarding if I had known then what I know now about having a clear vision.

—TOM LEE,
PRESIDENT AND CHIEF EXECUTIVE
OFFICER, NEWHALL
LAND & FARMING COMPANY

I wish I had known twenty-five years ago that my career did not have to grow only in a linear way, but could develop in more of a kaleidoscopic expansion.

As young men and women back then, we were taught the old rules of business—stick to the corporate ideals, find a mentor, don't go against the grain. If I'd known then that this mold only works for some people, and I was not one of them, I could have saved myself a lot of struggle.

Over time I learned that although the nail that sticks up is most likely the one to be struck, it is also most likely the one to get noticed.

The same holds true for the world of media in which I live. Twenty-five years ago who would have expected the Internet to become a reality, or that cable television would offer such a vast array of channels. The old models we learned from are either dying or are already extinct, and new ones are being created every day.

—ROBERT GOTTLIEB
EXECUTIVE VICE-PRESIDENT,
WILLIAM MORRIS AGENCY, INC.

Things
You'll
Be
Better
Off
Knowing

Be the first or the last into something.

After the Los Angeles riots, I was the first one to begin repairing and rebuilding my apartment houses and shopping centers in the city. And I have always been remembered for that.

And if you are last in, you have the advantage of learning from everyone else's mistakes.

But nobody cares if you are second. For example, can you name the last three Indy 500 second-place winners, or our last three vice-presidents?

Always be in front or at the end of the parade.

—JACK JONES
PRESIDENT, GREYSTONE
MANAGEMENT GROUP

Mⁱore than thirty years ago, someone told me when first starting a job, get the lay of the land before becoming a superstar.

The best approach is to first do a lot of observing; be as helpful as you can without being obnoxious, overly ambitious, or assertive. Try to become a team player as soon as possible. People will recognize your strengths without your broadcasting them all over the organization. If you have strong self-esteem, people will find that out without your telling them.

After you have been accepted in the organization, GO FOR IT. And, by the way, the way to receive a lot of recognition and credit is to give away as much of it as you can.

—GEORGE GREEN
PRESIDENT AND GENERAL
MANAGER, KABC LOS ANGELES

This is a hindsight that was really my foresight.

Back in 1972 I was offered the promotion to Creative Director. I told them I would take the job with one proviso—I would choose my own teams. I didn't ask for more money or a bigger office. I figured the money and square footage would come along in time, and it did.

Stokely Carmichael said, "All power comes from below." That sure makes sense when you are in charge of a gaggle of people. I choose "gaggle" because the word "gag" is in there, and the last part of "strangle," and sometimes I feel that way in my business of working with people and ideas.

After you pick your people, also give them feedback. If it's positive feedback, go overboard. If it's negative feedback, make it gentle. And always give credit.

Finally, surround yourself with "young uns." They have an energy and drive that's contagious. They just pull you along. Be prepared to spend lots of time with them and share your experiences. Just don't repeat old war stories more than three times or your listeners begin to wonder whether you've been cooking with aluminum pots.

—STANLEY BECKER
CREATIVE DIRECTOR, SAATCHI &
SAATCHI, NEW YORK

Things You'll Be Better Off Knowing

Do not resist change; it is eternal. Most of the things I have planned have evolved into something else, and not turned out as I expected. They have usually been better. God is always creating something new.

Have the courage to risk; it is essential. In my early years, I would spend time trying to create a stable base of support. But the base and conditions kept changing. Later on I learned to just "go for it." With hindsight, these are the times when truly positive things have happened in my professional or personal life.

The energy of taking a risk also creates an energy which seems to attract other people to help you achieve your goal.

—Dr. Karl Johnson
Senior Minister, Neighborhood
Church, Palos Verdes,
California

Greener pastures always have brown spots, too.

Nothing is perfect. There will always be someone who is your boss, has more money, or drives a better car.

No matter where you go, you will have clients or customers, and in turn, you will be somebody else's client. It's the way things are—sort of a "career food chain." It's that simple.

Stop worrying about it.

—SETH DINGLEY
PRINCIPAL, THE LAKERIDGE GROUP

Set your standards high and keep them high.

If you are interested in success, it's easy to set your standards in terms of other people's accomplishments. And then let other people measure you by those standards.

But the standards you set for yourself are always the more important. They should be higher than the standards anyone else would set for you, because in the end you have to live with yourself, and judge yourself, and feel good about yourself. And the best way to do that is to live up to your highest potential.

So set your standards high and keep them high, even if you think no one else is looking. Somebody

out there will *always* notice, even
if it's just you.

—Dianne Snedaker
President, Ketchum
Advertising/San Francisco

Things
You'll
Be
Better
Off
Knowing

Learn, earn, return—these are the three phases of life. The first third should be devoted to education, the second third to building a career and making a living, and the last third to giving back to others—returning something in gratitude. Each stage seems to be a preparation for the next one.

—JACK BALOUSEK
PRESIDENT & CHIEF OPERATING
OFFICER, TRUE NORTH
COMMUNICATIONS

Things You'll Be Better Off Knowing

Learn to distinguish between a mishap, a setback, and a tragedy.

Most bad things in life are mishaps. Setbacks are more serious but can be corrected. True tragedies are different. When you have experienced a tragedy you know the difference. And all things in life are put back in proportion and perspective.

Chances are most of the things you are anguishing over right now are mishaps. So relax.

—YOUNG PRESIDENTS'
ORGANIZATION WISDOM

From time to time be prepared to work for real jerks and be prepared to put up with it.

Don't be afraid to suck up. There's no guarantee that raw performance will get you anywhere.

Be aware that people you work for will have their own agendas that seldom have anything to do with you. So never assume that anything you want is on someone else's mind. If you want something, you have to tell people.

—STEVE SKINNER
SENIOR SEGMENT DIRECTOR,
PARAMOUNT TELEVISION
ENTERTAINMENT TONIGHT

Information is everything.

If you know more than anyone else, have thought more about it, and understand what truly drives your business, you will be successful.

But you have to figure out the appropriate time to make sure others know what you know. Demonstrating knowledge just to impress your superiors won't work; just use your knowledge and insight to do your job well.

And no matter what everyone says about the big picture, remember, God is in the details.

—JEFFREY KLEIN
PRESIDENT, LOS ANGELES TIMES
SAN FERNANDO VALLEY
& VENTURA COUNTY EDITIONS

Specialize in something. Become an expert. Really dig in and research some specific area. Become your company's focal point on something like the developments in new media, interactive communication, the impact of trends such as aging, or whatever. Know more than anyone else around you about some topic.

—ALLEN J. LARSON,
REGIONAL MEDIA DIRECTOR
EVANS GROUP ADVERTISING

Things You'll Be Better Off Knowing

Don't be afraid to make a career change.

Thinking back twenty-five years, I would have made a big mistake if I had not changed jobs. The company I left eventually went out of business and all the people still there had a very difficult time. Also, my wife contributed a lot to my success. Marry a person who wants to help with your career.

—GERALD A. FOUNTAIN
PRESIDENT, COOL
CARRIERS (USA) INC.

Be passionate about your work and have the integrity to stand up for your ideas. But also know when to compromise.

Without passion you will not be taken seriously. If you don't defend your ideas, no one else will either. When principle is involved, don't budge.

But there is another side to this also. There are very few real "absolutes" in life. Most matters involve taste or opinion, not principle. In these areas recognize that you can compromise. If you become someone who can never compromise, you will forfeit opportunities to those who can.

—MEL NEWHOFF
EXECUTIVE VICE PRESIDENT,
BOZELL WORLDWIDE

When you were born, you cried, and the world rejoiced.

May you live your life so that when you die, the world will cry, and you will rejoice.

—OLD MIDDLE EASTERN BLESSING

When you are eighty, sitting on that porch rocking, and looking back on your life, how will you feel? You won't have to answer to anybody but yourself . . . not your parents or your spouse or your business associates.

What did you do with this gift of living? It will be an important question to you then. So you should make it an important question now.

It is very important to have conviction behind your decisions. If you do not, someone else will fill the gap.

In the entertainment industry everyone you meet has two businesses, their own and "show business." Everyone has opinions about what movies and TV shows should be made, and about what they would have done differently with the ones already made. Nobody tells their doctor or lawyer how to run their business. Yet I run into "experts" almost every day. You have to trust yourself and your own judgment and then stay the course.

—ROWLAND PERKINS
FOUNDING PARTNER, CREATIVE
ARTISTS AGENCY, INC.

Every night ask yourself this question: "Have I made a profit for my employer today?" If the answer is "yes," you'll still have a job tomorrow. If it's "no," get your résumé together.

An employee can't merely be an expense to his or her company, but an investment that pays dividends. The bigger the dividend, the brighter your future.

Don't expect a raise because you've been at your job a given amount of time. Raises are given because you are worth more than you are currently being paid. Be worth more than you're making, and you'll soon be making what you're worth. So do more than you are asked; get to the office a little early; stay a little late; and if you run out of assignments, make up

your own. You might come up with
the big idea even your boss failed
to think of.

—BUDDY WEISS
PRESIDENT, WEISS ADVERTISING

Managing is your night job.

—JOHN DOONER
CHAIRMAN AND CHIEF EXECUTIVE
OFFICER, McCANN-ERICKSON
WORLDWIDE

John felt an agency manager's job was never to be behind his desk, but out and about—meeting with clients and his senior people trying to build the business. Paperwork—or what John called "managing"—was the manager's "night job."

You simply can't build relationships by phone or E-Mail. I don't care how sophisticated the information highway becomes. There will still be a need to "do it face-to-face." People trust people they see regularly.

Do not invest with friends or in deals promoted by friends without performing the same level of due diligence you would apply to an investment from an unknown source.

And when you enter into a business association, partnership, or joint venture with someone, look at all past business relationships of the prospective individual, the type of people with whom he or she associated, the period of the relationship, and the outcome. Look more at the results of the personal relationship than the business result.

—HOWARD M. KOFF
PRESIDENT AND CHIEF EXECUTIVE
OFFICER, WESTBURY FINANCIAL

N ever forget the value of a big idea. In our case, a single big idea can add $600 million to $700 million in sales in one year.

—JOHN MARTIN
PRESIDENT AND CHIEF EXECUTIVE
OFFICER, TACO BELL

We are in a totally new business world where telecommunications, interactivity, and the size of your RAM is as important as the size of your company. But no matter how sophisticated we become electronically, there will always be a priority placed on one person with a better idea. If you do everything right in your career, but don't champion big ideas, you are doomed to middle management.

Beware the myth of the gigantic brain.

This myth is the concept that somewhere at the base of larger companies or organizations is a group of people who know what the hell is going on. Generally it is a myth.

I wish someone had told me this earlier. I wish someone had told me to set my sights higher and worry less about the competition. That way, if I accomplished less than my goal, it would probably still be higher than my original target.

There are opportunities I missed because I thought only the big guys could pull it off—the ones with the gigantic brains. Then I realized that the "big guys" were just a group of small guys with

perhaps a few bigger ideas than mine.

Don't get intimidated by the world out there. Most people don't have a clue.

—DENNIS SCULLY
PRESIDENT, EXECUTIVE PAGE, LTD.

Here are my guidelines for writing a résumé based on reading thousands of them during fifty-five years in business.

1. Neatness counts. Typos count double—against. If a person doesn't present him- or herself with care, how can I expect better when they work for my firm?

2. I never look at letters of recommendation. As one of my colleagues once said, "I never saw a bad one."

3. I do look for clear, logical organization and simplicity, brevity, and honesty. Divide a résumé into headings such as business, education, outside activities, and personal. What more should I need to know?

4. I watch for signs of excessive or unrealistic performance claims. One young applicant had

been in an entry-level position with his former company when the firm won $10 million in new business. He took full credit.

5. Frequency and trends in job changes count. My father taught me that there are two serious mistakes a young person in business can make—changing jobs too often, and not changing jobs often enough.

Finally, I have never hired anyone who claimed to have worked for "Proctor & Gamble." Either the applicant was lying, or was not alert enough to check the spelling of his company name. Either sin is, to me, unforgivable.

—Monty McKinney
Former chairman, Chiat/Day
Doyle Dane Bernbach/West
Kresser/Craig

Build a wide range of relationships well beyond your comfort zone.

Life has taken me into new and unfamiliar areas, such as mergers and takeovers, seeking and obtaining a National Football League franchise, and dealing with civil rights issues. At every stage, the support of people I knew outside my area of expertise has been essential.

—JERRY RICHARDSON
OWNER AND FOUNDER,
CAROLINA PANTHERS
CHAIRMAN, FLAGSTAR
COMPANIES, INC.

Things You'll Be Better Off Knowing

Always be ready to walk away from a deal.

—CHARLIE COYLE
DIRECTOR, NEW YORK TIMES
MAGAZINE

There is a gambling expression: "If you can't lose, you can't win." You can't deal with someone if you can't walk away.

If you have to have the job, you can't negotiate your salary. If you have to keep the client to keep the office financially afloat, then you can't negotiate your commission. But if you can walk away, then you can approach the table seeking a win for both parties, or simply no deal.

THINGS YOU'LL BE NICER OFF KNOWING

Things You'll Be Nicer Off Knowing

Try to take a two-minute break between each meeting or phone call. This will prevent the tone of one event from infecting the next. You'll find that your analysis will be more accurate, your decisions much wiser, and your actions more appropriate.

—Susan J. Petersen
Publisher, Riverhead Books

Say thank you to three people.

—BILL BERNBACH
FOUNDER, DOYLE DANE
BERNBACH, INC.

Mr. Bernbach's point is simple—when something really good happens to you, such as getting a promotion or achieving a lifetime goal, stop for a few moments and think to whom you owe thanks.

It might be a teacher or professor, or a business mentor from twenty years ago, a family member who was there for you, or that person who gave you your first real break. Even if decades have passed, see if you can hunt down that person to simply say, "Thanks." It will remind you that you didn't do it all alone. It will keep you humble and be a real boon for those who've made a difference in your life.

Keep your ears and eyes open and your mouth shut. Tremendous sources of ingenuity are just waiting to be tapped all around you.

I have found that some of the most creative and exciting innovations have come from employees far removed from the action—but you have to ask and be available to listen. That is why leadership by an open door policy is part of our organization's culture.

And when every employee feels his or her opinions are valued, there is a sense of ownership in achieving company goals that you cannot buy at any price.

—DICK LOUGHLIN
FORMER PRESIDENT AND CHIEF
EXECUTIVE OFFICER, CENTURY 21
REAL ESTATE CORPORATION

Never react to a situation emotionally or impulsively. In my own experience, 90 percent of my success in merger and acquisition negotiations involved patience. Ninety percent of my failures involved lack of it. Don't reach for the holster. Take some time to think. Cool down. Wait twenty-four hours and then decide.

For example, when one of your associates walks into your office with a financial "surprise" three weeks before the end of your fiscal year, try to listen first. It may not be as bad as you think. Finally, when you can't make a decision between several alternatives and it's deadline time—guess what: move the deadline. Most due dates are really artificial and are therefore flexible.

Wait twenty-four hours before you react.

—SELWYN HERSON
CHIEF EXECUTIVE OFFICER,
THE WINDSOR PARK GROUP

I realize the importance of family and friends, of values and ideals, more than I may have twenty-five years ago. Achieving the appropriate value between personal life and business life and being comfortable with that balance is also the product of additional maturity.

—SID SHEINBERG
PRESIDENT, MCA INC.

Things You'll Be Nicer Off Knowing

Twenty-five years ago I wish someone had given me the Serenity Prayer. It asks to "grant me the serenity to accept the things that I cannot change; the courage to change the things I can," but most important, "the wisdom to know the difference" between the two.

—PAT RILEY
BASKETBALL COACH

N_o one cares how much you know until they know how much you care.

This actually is a quote first attributed to Dave Maister, a consultant to Ogilvy & Mather. It has always stayed with me. Another way of saying this is "Not calling is not caring."

Staying in touch with important clients means everything. It was hard for me to realize this when I first got into advertising. I felt sometimes that I didn't have anything to say or report, and calling might be an inconsiderate waste of my customers' time. Wrong. Clients need to see and hear from their suppliers. They need to know how much you care.

Don't worry about what to say— topics come up naturally, and your customer probably has his own list. And remember to listen first. Just prime the pump and then turn on your ears. These contacts invariably lead to priceless new information about how things are going.

And this rule also applies to new business. In our offices at Ogilvy there is a saying that goes "All things being equal, people will do business with people they like. All things not being equal, they still will."

—JERRY MCGEE
MANAGING DIRECTOR, OGILVY &
MATHER/LOS ANGELES

Develop your memory. It can be critically important. I can reflect back on experiences and opportunities lost simply because I could not remember a name, a place, or even a number, and that meant the difference between success and failure.

—GREG ECONN
PRESIDENT, JAMES ECONN & CO.

Sounds simple enough. Among the most important rules is remembering someone's name. It is said that the sweetest sound in any language is the sound of your own name correctly pronounced.

Help the other person out, too. When you meet someone again, don't play a game to see if they remember your name. Put your hand out and say your name out loud. They will always say, "Of course, I remember you," but half the time they didn't, and will secretly appreciate your help.

Kindness can prove to be the single most valuable trait in building professional relationships. Take a personal interest in colleagues and business contacts. It will produce opportunities too numerous to count. And kindness doesn't cost a dime.

—THOMAS A. MALOOF
PRESIDENT AND CHIEF EXECUTIVE
OFFICER, PRIMEHEALTH
OF SOUTHERN CALIFORNIA

The real key to success in life is putting others first: your family, business associates, friends, and customers.

I believe we enter this world as relatively selfish creatures and spend our entire lives trying to become less so.

When I was first married, my wife and I lived in England. My focus was almost entirely on my career. I thought I was a good husband because I put bread on the table. I ignored my wife's emotional needs living far away from home. I spent too little time on her feelings and too much time on my own.

—ROBERT J. BAUER
PRESIDENT, RAY COOK
GOLF COMPANY

Always be on time.

Respect for someone else's time is the greatest compliment. Think about it. The most valuable—and perishable—thing we own is our time. When someone abuses it by being late to a meeting with us, it should be considered an insult. And, in reverse, we owe people the courtesy of respecting their time, and being on time ourselves. Better an hour early than five minutes late.

Generally, the higher you go in any organization, the more courteous the reception and the more on time the meetings. Real leaders don't keep other people waiting.

—Walter Merryweather, Former Chief Executive Officer, Illinois Meat Company

There is no truth to the maxim, "Nice guys finish last."

I was once told it is not important to be liked, it is important to be respected. The two are not mutually exclusive. Some people think they are respected when they actually are feared.

Be yourself. Be secure in your knowledge, your beliefs, your sensitivity to others, and your morality. Role models are important, but don't try to emulate someone whose style and values are not compatible with yours.

It's true that many assholes get to the top, but you don't have to be one to succeed.

—SIMON M. KORNBLIT
FORMER EVP, WORLDWIDE
MARKETING, UNIVERSAL PICTURES

Things You'll Be Nicer Off Knowing

When someone close to you has a tragedy, don't just send flowers or a card . . . send yourself.

Don't avoid people when they have a death in their family. Get on a plane or in your car and go. They won't remember what you said, but they will never forget you came. Be there again for that person in three months or six months, when everyone else will have forgotten and moved on. This is when real friendship counts most.

Also, always say the name of the deceased person. Boom it right out loud. Everyone else will tiptoe around in silence, avoiding the name as if the person never existed. And that can hurt the most.

—HARRY CHANDIS
FORMER PRESIDENT,
BUSINESS PUBLICATIONS,
ZIFF-DAVIS PUBLISHING

You have no enemies. There are just some people or groups whose dreams, desires, and goals happen to be in conflict with yours.

So don't hate. Analyze every situation and see how you can obtain the best possible results, while at the same time your adversary can achieve a certain amount of success, too, at the least expense to you.

—PETER CALOYERAS
CHAIRMAN OF THE BOARD,
MAGNETIKA, INC.

The key to a successful personal and professional life is to always be yourself and not what others expect you to be. Say what you mean and be who you are. It has worked for me.

—AL NIRENSTEIN
PRESIDENT, RODNEY STRONG
VINEYARDS

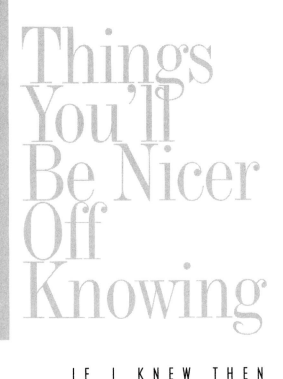
Things You'll Be Nicer Off Knowing

IF I KNEW THEN

Twenty-five years ago I didn't know the meaning of the word "balance." Now I know.

It means learning to say NO to yet another meeting, association dinner, sales pitch, or "It would be nice if you could attend. . . ."

I know now that balance means saying YES to leaving the office early to watch your son's Little League game, and without your cellular phone. It means arriving late to the office because you wanted to drive your daughter to class; or not coming in at all so you can do something that can't be done on the weekend, and is important to you.

What a difference twenty-five years makes.

—BRAD BALL
PRESIDENT, DAVIS, BALL &
COLOMBATTO

Give serendipity a chance. You don't have to plan or try to focus every step in your life.

I wish I had taken advantage of the opportunity to just learn about as many things as possible when I was younger. I wish I had just listened to all the World History and World Culture courses, instead of just trying to get an "A" on the exam. Stay loose early. You spend the rest of your life narrowing your focus.

—DR. CONDOLEEZZA RICE
PROVOST, STANFORD UNIVERSITY

The true secret weapon to succeed in this life is this: if you want to be first, go to the back of the line.

I'm talking about the Golden Rule: "Do unto others as you would have them do unto you." It has been around for thousands of years for a reason. It is so powerful, so foolproof, it should be made illegal.

To employ it faithfully every day is to guarantee an abundance of peace, happiness, spiritual joy, and material wealth beyond your wildest dreams. Treat your clients like they are the most important people on earth. Cherish your spouse as if he or she were royalty. In working with fellow employees, place their priorities ahead of yours. Follow this rule with competitors, neighbors, assistants, sons, daughters, waitresses, and yes, even attorneys.

Place these people ahead of yourself sincerely in your thoughts and actions, and you can stop worrying about life. Why? Because these people will reward you and take care of you with astounding power and abundance. The love that you spend on others will be reflected back onto you like a tidal wave. A tidal wave that will engulf you in a life of happiness that no man could ever achieve alone.

Once you know this secret, there is no other way to live.

—Mark Choate
Senior Portfolio Manager,
Smith Barney, Inc.

Turn the light switch off when you leave.

—DICK RUUD
PRESIDENT, RUUD & PARTNERS

This hindsight is a simple "memory trick." When you enter your office in the morning and turn your light switch on, think of it as also turning yourself on. The engine is up and running and in full gear.

But when you leave at night, turn both your lights and your business self off. Leave the troubles on your desk behind you. Don't take them home. Keep your life in healthy balance.

Lights on. Lights off. Bulbs and people don't burn out as quickly that way.

"If I had my life to live over, I would dare to make more mistakes next time. I would relax. I would limber up. I would be sillier than I've been this time. I would take fewer things seriously, and I would take more chances. I'd take more trips; I'd climb more mountains and I'd swim more rivers. I would eat more ice cream, and less beans. I would perhaps have more actual troubles, but I'd have fewer imaginary ones.

"You see, I am one of those people who lived sensibly and sanely, hour after hour, day after day. Oh, I've had my moments, but if I had it to do over again, I'd have more of them. In fact, I'd try to have nothing else—just moments— one after another instead of living so many years ahead.

"I've been one of those persons

who never goes anywhere without
a thermometer, a hot-water bottle,
a raincoat, and a parachute. If I
had my life to live over, I would
start barefoot earlier in the
spring, and I would stay that way
later in the fall. I would go to
more dances. I would ride more
merry-go-rounds. I would pick
more daisies."

—NADINE STAIR

THINGS YOU MIGHT REALLY WISH YOU'D KNOWN

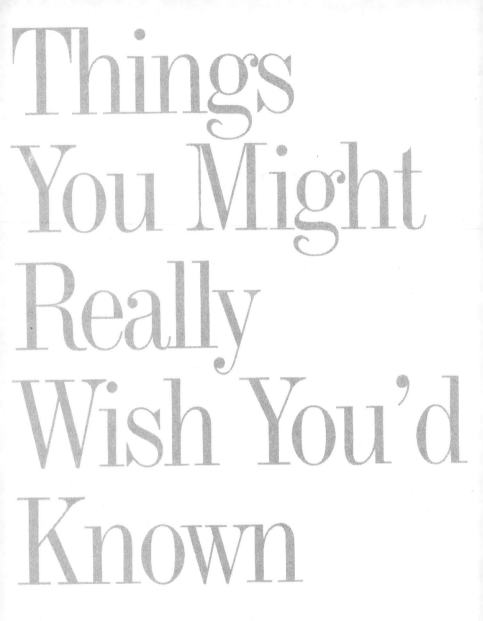

Things You Might Really Wish You'd Known

Twenty-five years ago I wish someone had told me about the exponential factor of time: that every year over forty years of age goes twice as fast, and every year over fifty goes ten times as fast.

—HAROLD EVANS
PUBLISHER, RANDOM HOUSE

You cannot take the money you saved with you when you die, but you can take the money you gave away.

You cannot take the food you stored up, but you can take the food you shared.

What you gave away to help others you take with you. What you kept you leave behind.

—Reverend Dr. Charles L. Heuser
Author, Pilgrimage in Faith

As a young tiger in 1954 I embraced a "success formula" that remains valid and unchanged today: Always give 110 percent effort. Develop people skills. Remain the student. Be loyal to my employer. Keep an unwavering commitment to values.

Yet, in hindsight, what I didn't focus on at the start of the race forty years ago were the personal intangibles that seem to make the thin difference between those who fulfill their potential and those who don't.

Judgment—which means not just making the right decision but making it at the right time.

Sensitivity—to others all the time. I learned that not everybody approached things with my eager-beaver style, but that they could be even more effective by being sensi-

Things You Might Really Wish You'd Known

tive and really caring about other peoples' needs.

High octane enthusiasm—for everything you do. If you want to be alone, if you want to be ignored, don't bother to smile.

Persistence—there is no task that doesn't guarantee problems and obstacles. Only those who doggedly persist will obtain their goals. On the fifty-fifth anniversary of Winston Churchill's graduation from Groton he gave the commencement address. Gripping the podium, he uttered three words and sat down: PERSIST. PERSIST. PERSIST.

—PEN TUDOR
CHAIRMAN OF THE EXECUTIVE
COMMITTEE, ADWEEK

Twenty-five years ago I wish someone had told me to formally put pen to paper and write down my own personal vision statement.

My own statement starts with an awareness that we live in a world of abundance rather than scarcity. There is enough for all of us—one person's gain need not be another's loss. From this comes my own personal vision: "To love one another." Yours might be very different. The key is that my statement clarifies for me *the next right thing to do.* It really drives my decisions every day. So should yours.

—BARBARA BOOLS
PRESIDENT, BOOLS & ASSOCIATES

Things You Might Really Wish You'd Known

I wish someone had told me that it was going to turn out all right.

I worried myself almost into craziness about money, about getting fired, about ever being successful. I had an invalid sister to support and the burdens were heavy. I wish there had been somebody to say, "Kiddo, if you work very, very hard and just pick yourself up and go on when you get fired—which I sometimes did—and take advantage of anything anybody asks you to do, you'll be okay."

I did those things sort of by *instinct* but it wouldn't have hurt to have a real-live cheer-up team in the room. We're talking fifty years ago. Twenty-five years ago *Cosmo* was doing gorgeously and I didn't really need a cheer up team then.

It couldn't be any tougher now

than it was for "my crowd" just coming out of the Depression in 1940—ninety job applicants for one job. But if you don't aim too high—head in the clouds and visions of sugarplums—and just do the boring work in front of you as conscientiously as you know how, it catapults you to the next plateau—in that company or another.

Get in the habit of being a professional. Half of success is thinking that what you are doing has got to be done the best anybody ever did it, even if it is filing and redoing an address book. Self-discipline will get you everywhere (she said sanctimoniously!).

—HELEN GURLEY BROWN
EDITOR IN CHIEF, COSMOPOLITAN

Keep in touch with friends. Don't let those ships sail away.

You never know when other people can help you, or just be there for you. Looking back, I regret that I did not stay closely in touch with people from my twenties. These are people I worked alongside at one time. Later on I read about them in trade journals, but no longer knew them. Too much time had passed. It was no longer possible to call up and say "Hi, it's Dave."

Someone once said, "A good friend is like a good dog—both need to be taken out and exercised regularly."

—DAVE KING
DIRECTOR OF MARKETING, BLUE
SHIELD OF CALIFORNIA

Follow what you love to do. If you don't, you will probably backtrack later in your life to reclaim it anyway.

My parents were shaped by the Depression. Their priorities stressed security, not the passionate pursuit of dreams. I was urged to become a teacher because it offered security. As I look back, the things that I loved when young were design and horticulture. Yet I wasn't sure enough of myself to pursue these until I was thirty-five. Don't make that mistake.

Do what you love even if it doesn't have the flash of big money or the veneer of prestige. If you scratch the surface of what you don't love, you will find it empty and live the "I wish I hads." But if you do what you love, you won't be able to get enough of it in a whole lifetime.

Finally, pass your belief in self-discovery on to your children. Look at them through their talents instead of your desires for them.

—Jacqueline Ignon
Landscape architect

Things You Might Really Wish You'd Known

Power is always at play behind the scenes. Some use it. Some abuse it. Too many women tend to walk away from it. Don't. Power with benevolence and without machismo is the art of leadership.

—JEAN CRAIG
FOUNDER, KRESSER/CRAIG
ADVERTISING

Things You Might Really Wish You'd Known

Twenty-five years ago I wish someone had told me to strike a better balance between the cautious risk aversion taught by America's larger corporations and the heart-stopping risk acceptance practiced by its most daring entrepreneurs.

As I look back on my career I do not regret mistakes, but I do regret opportunities missed—the opportunity to grow a business faster when I had strong financial backing; the still-birth of good ideas I wouldn't risk undertaking; and the reluctance to put personal capital and reputation behind ideas that had reasonable promise of blossoming.

—RICHARD H. BURKE
PRESIDENT, BURKE,
FOX & COMPANY

I wish someone had told me when I came out of law school, all set to practice, that I needed immediately to find somebody to practice on.

—MORT JANKLOW
CHAIRMAN, JANKLOW &
NESBIT ASSOCIATES

In hospital emergency rooms nurses have a saying, "Watch one, do one, teach one." This refers to the fast pace of the profession and the need to learn quickly, then jump right in to practice what you learned on a real live patient, and then pass it on just as quickly to someone else. Notice that learning is only the first one-third of the job. The real key is putting that learning into practice.

It applies to any profession or business. You can't just read about how to change a tire, ride a bike, write a contract, start a business, or perform open-heart surgery. You need to perform the skill to perfect the skill.

I turn around deeply troubled or bankrupt companies for a living.

It doesn't matter what business they are in. I have found that the same five steps apply every time. I wish someone had told me this twenty-five years ago instead of having to learn it the hard way. Here they are:

Step One: Grab the cash. Most companies in trouble are also hemorrhaging. Cut deals with vendors. Sell assets. Stop payments. Do whatever you need to do to corral the liquid assets immediately. Do not delegate this function until it is well in hand. Until you have done this you are not in control.

Step Two: Freeze the expenses. Don't worry about revenue for now. Just lock down the expenses. Cut everything you can, including executive salaries. Let them feel the crisis and share in the solutions.

Step Three: Interview everyone you can. All the information about what is wrong and what should be done is already in house.

Step Four: Formulate a strategy for the direction of the company. You are better off with a half-right strategy now, than a perfectly right strategy in six months. By then it will be too late.

Step Five: Draw up the "ideal" organization chart to reflect the minimum necessary staff to implement the strategy. When you do this, start fresh. Ignore the people who now work for the company. After you have the ideal organization chart, go back and slot in the people you have if they fit somewhere. Most managers take the existing

staff and try to find a job for them. This is disaster. Lay out the organization first. If people don't fit, get rid of them. Sounds cold, but executives are paid to execute.

That's it. Works every time.

—Alfred Jay Moran, Jr.
Chief Executive Officer,
Gérant Companies, Inc.

Find a lawyer and build a relationship early in life, before you
need one. Someday you will need
one suddenly, and you won't have
time to look around. I guarantee it.

—ANONYMOUS

Things You
Might Really
Wish You'd
Known

THINGS YOU'LL BE GRATEFUL

TO KNOW

Things You'll Be Grateful To Know

I'm actually pleased that what I know now I didn't know twenty-five years ago. If I had, I would have worried about whether I would find a job, succeed, and have a satisfying career. But, when I got out of college, none of those things seemed to be important. We just put one step in front of the other and moved forward. Women weren't expected to rise to the top of any business ladder, and consequently I had no stress at all thinking about my future.

I wanted to be able to do something I loved, to wake up in the morning and look forward to going to work (as my father did), and to have a career that gave me time to spend with my children.

I can't say that I planned my career climb. The events just happened and looking backward, I am grateful that I never heard the term "career path" when I was twenty-two. Young people today put too much stress and pressure on themselves and forget that if you work very hard, do the best that you can do, stay out of office politics, and enjoy your life, you need no rigid outline for success.

—ELLEN LEVINE
EDITOR IN CHIEF,
GOOD HOUSEKEEPING

Things
You'll
Be
Grateful
to
Know

Laugh with yourself and enjoy your own company. Create your own life. Don't let others define it for you. Whatever you do, do it for your own reasons—because it serves your plan and pleases yourself. Let go of people or things that drag you down. Remember, you are the driver. Stay in the driver's seat so you can stop, back up, accelerate, or turn. Keep your independence of thought. Enjoy your imagination and dreams. Forgive yourself. Take time for people, especially the people you love. Enjoy learning and embrace change. Life is a wondrous gift. Enjoy the ride.

—STEVE ROBBINS
PRESIDENT, ROBBINS BROS.
THE ENGAGEMENT RING STORE

B
eware the beige people syndrome.

—Thom Miller
Former president,
Ketchum Advertising/New York

Thom Miller has "clubbed" with the best of them. After years of this, he concluded he was tired of rep ties and cardigan sweaters, and yearned for people who didn't care what your title was, how much you made last year, or where you went to school.

Beige people who blend in and stand for nothing are rarely anybody's first choice. Don't be afraid to take a stand or to be controversial. You may make a few enemies, but better friends. Fit in, but don't sell out.

Don't count on appreciation of assets until cashed. Deal only in reality.

On any windfall—bonus, commission, sale of an asset, etc.— put away at least 75 percent in a low- or non-risk investment and spend only the interest. Then understand and monitor closely your personal cash flow.

If it's "too good to be true," be careful and take a closer look. Understand that any good investment or venture can be either the result of luck or smarts—and it's difficult to "reproduce" luck.

In my case, I thought I had a great, balanced real estate portfolio, but a recession wiped out 40 percent of its value—which happened to be most of my equity.

—BILL LENNARTZ
PRESIDENT AND CHIEF EXECUTIVE
OFFICER, SCITEQ ELECTRONICS,
INC.

If a customer calls, and I consider it an interruption, I know I have to take some time off to adjust my attitude.

—DON KEOUGH
RETIRED PRESIDENT AND COO,
THE COCA-COLA COMPANY

Think about your customer's needs instead of your own, and the business will take care of itself. Understand how your clients make money, and help them make more, and your income will take care of itself. Clients or customers are the reason for success, not an interruption in the day.

The seeker goes to the mountain top and asks the learned one:

"Where does wisdom come from?"

"Good judgment."

"Where does good judgment come from?"

"Experience."

"Where does experience come from?"

"Bad judgment."

—OLD SUFI STORY
DR. PIERRE MORNELL
PSYCHIATRIST AND AUTHOR

Pierre adds a side note to his hindsight: "Beware of sixty-year-olds, like myself, giving you advice about where wisdom comes from. You're the expert on your own experience . . . so trust yourself."

I wish someone had told me that marriage is not a 50/50 proposition. Don't be a scorekeeper.

I have been married for thirty-four very happy years, and in all that time it is difficult to remember when my husband and I each gave 50 percent. Needs vary. Some years you find yourself giving 90 or even 100 percent to your relationship; but recognize that there will inevitably be a time when you will need to receive more than your share. Then your spouse will be there for you.

Marriage is about love and sharing and teamwork. Give out of love. Don't worry about "what's in it for me," or "now you owe me." Don't keep score. You'll never be sorry.

—DEBBIE CONLON
FOUNDER, INTERIORS BY DESIGN

In thinking about things I wish someone had told me years ago, I thought of some of the principles that have guided us at Mattel since I took over in 1987.

1. Profitability is our top priority. The main reason we all work "long and hard" is to enhance shareholder value. People tend to say they work to pay bills or put food on the table or whatever. Those items are important but the major reason we are working is to increase profitability for our shareholders.

2. People make the difference. If you have excellent people working for you, it makes your job so much easier. Recruit intelligent, dedicated, creative personnel, and the business will respond . . . if you let those people do their jobs.

3. Be involved in community projects. Nothing is more reward-

John's focus on profitability may be misunderstood and seem insensitive: an emphasis on profit at the expense of people. And yet just the reverse is true. Profitability is number one on the list because it makes everything else possible.

In 1987 John Amerman took over a company that was close to bankruptcy and made it into one of the great turn-around success stories in American business. In a few years Mattel stock tripled and by 1995 the company had become the largest and most profitable toy company in the world. By his focus on profitability first, John was able to achieve all his other objectives: hire good people, be involved in community projects, and have fun.

ing than reaching out to activities outside the company. I don't believe the vast majority of young people starting out in business understand this requirement.

4. Have fun. When you think about it, we come to work early in the morning and stay until it is late at night. If we don't get some fun out of the business, then we would have a very dreary existence. Having fun is one of the most important principles for sustained growth in any organization.

—JOHN AMERMAN
CHAIRMAN AND CHIEF EXECUTIVE
OFFICER, MATTEL TOYS

Capsule Course in
Human Relations

1. Five most important words in the English language:

"I am proud of you."

2. Four most important words:

"What is your opinion?"

3. Three most important words:

"If you please."

4. Two most important words:

"Thank you."

5. Least important word: "I."

—ROBERT W. WOODRUFF
RETIRED CHAIRMAN,
THE COCA-COLA COMPANY

Things You'll Be Grateful to Know

Listen to that still small voice inside you.

If you do not live your life completely, realizing goals you hold to be worthwhile, making your unique contribution to the world, nobody ever will. Your song will die with you.

Many of us have discovered what we want to do with our lives. We have a purpose that resonates to the very core of our being. Somehow our lives will never be complete unless we answer this calling. But we refrain . . . the "still small voice" whispers a dream . . . but later that day or the next our vision starts to fade . . . immersed in the practical, our dreams and aspirations seem uncertain and perhaps a bit foolish.

We plod the highway of conformity, each following the other. We seek what others seek—comfort, security, money, power, pleasure. We are not alone, but only a stranger to our better selves. Years leave wrinkles upon the skin. But this loss of enthusiasm leaves wrinkles upon the soul.

It is impossible to tell another what path he should follow. Only you, in stillness and humility, can listen to that still small voice. Success and happiness are not distant goals to capture and hold. They happen incidentally while you are fulfilling yourself.

—MICHAEL LYNBERG, AUTHOR
FROM THE GIFT OF GIVING

Never attend a meeting unless you know when it's going to end. Of the thousands of hours we all spend in business meetings, precious few are as productive as they could be. Over the course of a career, this can easily add up to years.

An effective way to bring discipline to this otherwise wasteful ritual is to establish an end time in addition to a start time for every meeting you chair or attend. If you are calling the meeting, this practice immediately sends the message to your colleagues that you value their time. If you are attending a meeting called by someone else, it tells them that your time must be respected.

Two corollaries: first, always have an agenda, no matter how large or small your meeting, and follow it rigorously. Second—and this is my personal favorite—any meeting that lasts more than twenty minutes isn't worth having in the first place.

—PETER BROWN
CREATIVE DIRECTOR, ANITA
SANTIAGO ADVERTISING

Things
You'll Be
Grateful to
Know

There was a brilliant television commercial for alcoholism awareness done by Jim and others in the late eighties at Doyle Dane Bernbach.

In the commercial there is an elephant in the house but everybody in the family ignores it. The children play around the trunk, the mother vacuums around the leg and so forth. The idea is that alcoholism in a family is like an elephant in the room—everybody knows it is there, but they all pretend it doesn't exist.

I picked up on this phrase and used it myself. I found that in many meetings there were "elephants in the room," issues that were very real but went unaddressed because people were more comfortable pretending they didn't exist.

I would open meetings with a simple question, "Okay, before we get started, are there any

B eware of the elephant in the room.

—JIM HALLOWES
PRESIDENT, HALLOWES
PRODUCTIONS

Things You'll Be Grateful to Know

elephants in the room?" Occasionally I'd name the elephants myself: "I know that Sue and Dave are having a fight over who gets the corner office, and I want to get it out on the table so it doesn't become an elephant later on."

The point is simply to identify hidden agendas and neutralize them as much as possible. The acknowledgment of a problem publicly goes a long way toward solving it.

Success is waking up in the morning, whoever you are, wherever you are, however old or young, and bounding out of bed because there's something out there that you love to do, that you believe in, that you're good at—something that's bigger than you are, and you can hardly wait to get at it again today.

—WHIT HOBBS
COLUMNIST

Don't *tell* people. Instead, ask what they think and listen to their answers. A constructive two-way communication process results in the "receiver" believing that he or she is valued. After all, we all tend to support and embrace what we help create.

Twenty-five years ago, some wonderful people helped me with this advice. They included me, they valued me, they stretched and supported me. I was truly a participant in my own learning process—not the recipient of a "telling" process.

Benjamin Franklin captured it when he said, "If you state an opinion to me in a dogmatic manner, which is in direct opposition to my thought, and you imply no room to negotiate, then I must conclude, in order to protect my own self-esteem, that you are wrong and will immediately undertake to prove you wrong. On the other hand, if you state your opinion as a hypothesis, with evidence of a willingness to discuss and explore, I will most likely undertake to prove you correct."

—JAMES M. EDLER
MANAGER, ORGANIZATIONAL CHANGE,
AIRCRAFT ENGINE DIVISION,
GENERAL ELECTRIC COMPANY

Things
You'll
Be
Grateful
to
Know

Celebrate publicly. Cry alone. Years ago I wish someone had told me that there is no such thing as "off the record." It is simply good practice not to show weakness to others. Don't quit a job to search for a job. And don't open up to people with your inner feelings of doubt or hurt—they don't really want to hear it. The more popular expression for this is "never let them see you sweat."

Nobody feels sorry for you for more than an hour, but they will never forget your moment of vulnerability. The problem with letting down your guard is that when things are better again, and you run into the person you shared with, he or she will remember you "back when."

There is also no such thing as "in strictest confidence" among casual friends or with the press. In journalism the phrase "not for attribution" usually means they will use everything you tell them, but not your name.

Finally, always be cautious of the person who comes to you with a line like: "Now, I'm not supposed to tell anyone, but I think you should know." If that person will tell you someone else's secret, he will do the same thing with what you tell him.

—CRAIG CAMPBELL
CHIEF EXECUTIVE OFFICER, EVANS
GROUP/LOS ANGELES

IF I KNEW THEN

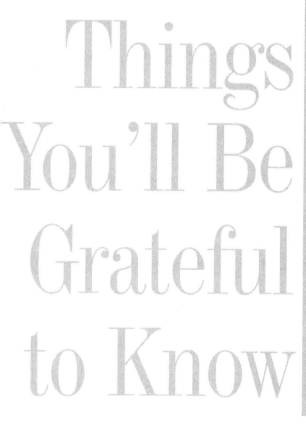

Men and women are different. Even though you love your spouse, every man also needs to have at least one true male friend.

—ROSS HUNTLEY
DENTIST PHILOSOPHER

Things
You'll Be
Grateful
to Know

Wear muddy boots.

—KANSAS AGRICULTURAL
ADVERTISING AGENCY'S NEW
BUSINESS PHILOSOPHY

I have made new business presentations to lots of blue-chip companies. And I have seen new business done well by the biggest ad agencies in the world. But I have never seen it done better than by a little shop in Kansas.

At the beginning of the meeting the head of the agency reaches under the table and brings out a pair of muddy boots and puts them in the center of the conference-room table. "Now folks," he says, "this is our business philosophy at this agency. If you hire us, we will get our boots muddy. We will walk your fields with you. We will get as deeply involved in your business as you are. And we will thoroughly understand your problems before we try to create advertising solutions for you."

I wish somebody had told me early on that one of the keys to success is breaking the rules rather than following them.

During my twenties I would occasionally break the rules, and it would pay off. For instance, when I entered a contest to "write about your goals for the future" I decided it might be more attention-getting to write "Why I have no goals." I won.

Unfortunately, when I would break the rules this way, I'd scare myself and then start behaving again. Eventually I wised up.

Today I know that the best way to come up with innovative ideas and creative projects is to be bold, gutsy, imaginative—and not to do what "they" told me to.

—KATE WHITE
EDITOR IN CHIEF, REDBOOK
MAGAZINE AND AUTHOR OF
WHY GOOD GIRLS DON'T
GET AHEAD . . . . BUT
GUTSY GIRLS DO

Things You'll Be Grateful to Know

THINGS LEARNED THE
HARD WAY

Things
Learned
The
Hard
Way

Sometimes you find yourself between a rock and a rock. That's the time to cut your losses.

—JIM LINDSEY
FORMER PRESIDENT,
PEPSI-COLA BOTTLING
SAN DIEGO AND SAN BERNARDINO

I was in an investment with Jim and others when he offered this advice. We were indeed "between rocks" and there wasn't even a "hard place," and we all cut our losses. I look upon what it cost as tuition for lessons learned, and some of the best money I ever spent.

Twenty-five years ago I wish someone had told me that vacation time is as important as any other function in the race for success.

Do not confuse a few three-day weekends here and there with a real vacation. Leave everything and go with your family for some time away together. Go anywhere, as long as it is away from the office.

It is easy to believe that everything may fall apart if you're not there, but it usually doesn't; and those things that absolutely can't wait for you can.

As a young entrepreneur I was guilty of this. For the first seven years after I started my business I never took a vacation. Then, after one short week at the beach, my outlook improved, my energy level went up, and I was bursting with new ideas and totally refreshed. And as a bonus I had a renewed appreciation for my family.

—LEE WELDON
FORMER CHIEF EXECUTIVE
OFFICER, KAL/HEALTHWAY CORP.

Say "no" when you mean "no." This can be the biggest time saver in your life.

—LINDA LoRe
PRESIDENT, GIORGIO BEVERLY
HILLS

Try saying "no" more often. Think of it as a gift to yourself. Most people will respect your decision, and not push it. It feels a little awkward at first, because you have been taught to say "yes" to be polite. But saying "no" is honest and straightforward and winds up saving everyone's time.

The alternative is to say "yes," and then become more and more miserable later on as an occasion approaches on your calendar and you try to think of a reason to cancel. I know you have been there.

Looking back, I have three hindsights to pass on.

1. Most business ventures take twice as long, cost twice as much, and are twice as difficult as your most conservative estimate. And the return is usually half of what you expected. If that still looks good to you, go for it.

2. It's not a good idea to have senior people who report to you also become members of your Board of Directors. It is a set-up for conflict when you review them, and they review you.

3. There are very few cases of an amicable divorce. It's very tough on the kids and your spouse will own more of you than you could ever imagine today. Remember, the worst reconciliation is better than the best divorce. Trust me on this one.

—MARK HEBNER
PRESIDENT, GUARDIAN X-RAY

Bill Lupien's advice covers both compensation and risk.

By having someone else negotiate your compensation, you take yourself out of that incredibly awkward position of trying to both please your boss and play "hard ball" at the same time—an impossible situation. An intermediary provides a buffer, yet can drive a much harder bargain and probably *double* the final package.

In terms of risk taking, the courage to stick your neck out is an important mark of a leader. If you aren't stretching, you aren't growing. And when you stretch, you take risks, sometimes get fired, fail miserably, or whatever. I've always liked an ad from United Technologies Corporation run years ago in *The Wall Street Journal*. It is reprinted here with the company's permission:

1. Always have someone else negotiate your compensation for you. Unless you are embarrassed, you aren't asking for enough.

2. Expect to fail miserably 30 percent of the time.

—BILL LUPIEN
CHIEF EXECUTIVE OFFICER,
MITCHUM, JONES & TEMPLETON,
INC.

Don't Be Afraid to Fail

You've failed
many times,
although you may not
remember.
You fell down
the first time
you tried to walk.
You almost drowned
the first time
you tried to
swim, didn't you?
Did you hit the
ball the first time
you swung a bat?
Heavy hitters,
the ones who hit the
most home runs,
also strike
out a lot.
R. H. Macy
failed seven
times before his

*store in New York
caught on.
English novelist
John Creasey got
753 rejection slips
before he published
564 books.
Babe Ruth struck out
1330 times,
but he also hit
714 home runs.
Don't worry about
failure.
Worry about the
chances you miss
when you don't
even try.*

I wish someone had told me about OPM—other people's money. Or, to put it in more businesslike terms, "equity financing." What I mean is a good clear understanding of raising capital to grow a business.

—ED JUSTICE
PRESIDENT, JUSTICE
BROTHERS, INC.

Things
Learned
The
Hard
Way

Always get the best legal and accounting advice! If you have to pay more, it will be worth it. Never stick with your "old" accountant or attorney when complex issues confront you.

Twenty-five years ago during negotiations for a merger of our company, we used the same "old" accountant and the same "old" attorney who had grown up with the business. They just did not have the expertise to handle a complex merger. As the deal was completed, we thought we "merged" but later found out we were "sold."

It was a devastating blow to our family, and I never forgot the error.

—ANONYMOUS

When I was nineteen I thought I was immortal. I thought I would live forever. A terrible accident brought a new perspective to my life and the way I lived thereafter.

I realized that death was something very much linked to life, and that the only two true facts in life are that you were born one day and that you will die some day. What happens in between depends on your own way of living.

Having been so near death, there is only one thing that kept me going . . . that is love for my family. In extreme limit survival situations, the body and the mind are already exhausted and finished. For me I was able to survive seventy-two days on a glacier in the high Andes because of the thought that I had to go back to my father and sister. My mother

Fernando Parrado's story of courage and survival is told in the book and film *Alive*.

and younger sister were killed in the plane crash. No training or physical stamina could have saved me. My only strength came from thinking about my family. It gave me power and the chance to live again.

Every day I try to give my family all the love that I can. There is nothing in life as important. We all know that when we start our final journey, the things that made our life worthwhile are not material, but things of feelings. So try to enjoy the simple things. These are the ones you will miss if you are ever in a life-threatening situation.

—FERNANDO PARRADO
PRESIDENT M.R.C. LTD,
MONTEVIDEO, URUGUAY

Twenty-five years ago I wish someone had told me three things:

1. Network your heart out. Go to every event, conference, or party, no matter how tired you are. The contact you make when you least expect it, can impact your entire career . . . or perhaps even lead to romance.

2. Pay off your credit cards every month—at least the minimum—no matter what. Don't let the month go by without paying something—or it will catch up and haunt you.

3. Consider that the "glass ceiling" may be partly your fault. As the president of a leading U.S. executive search firm specializing in minorities and women, I see too many candidates who need a simple and blunt talking to—regarding professional business appearance. The solution for both men and

women may, in part, be a better tailored suit, complementary blouse or shirt, the right tie, and polished shoes. When seeking an executive position, the successful candidate must truly look the part.

—BETSY BERKHEMER-CREDAIRE
PRESIDENT AND FOUNDER,
DIVERSITY SEARCH PARTNERS, INC.

Things Learned The Hard Way

Get your retirement money now.

Many of us in our fifties and sixties today got fooled. We were raised to believe that there was some kind of lifelong pact between our employer and ourselves.

When we got out of college there were plenty of jobs. And corporations talked about training programs, career advancement, and even pension. Imagine someone talking to a twenty-one-year-old about the pension plan.

Today there are no promises. "Lifetime employment" is something our fathers and grandfathers had. Don't count on it.

So get your money up front. Every time you have an option to take a cash bonus, ask your company to use it to buy a tax-deferred annuity of some kind. When you buy these in your twenties and thirties, they are dirt cheap because of your life expectancy. So for twenty or thirty thousand dollars at age thirty, you might guarantee a million when you retire.

It is very hard for most younger people to think thirty years ahead. But if you make the effort to save now, you have the most wonderful thing later on: the independence and peace of mind that comes from knowing your retirement is taken care of—even if your employer hands you a pink slip when you least expect it.

—Anonymous

Twenty-five years ago I wish someone had told me to make the first loss the last loss. This means don't chase after a bad decision and try to rectify it or defend it. Face up to problems and fix them or bail out.

During my years at Chrysler, managers told me to either divorce myself from bad situations or hide. But with the company then in serious financial trouble I couldn't play that game, and quickly learned that I earned real respect from my superiors if I came to them straight up, often with a recommendation to eliminate a project. Of course, it's a good idea to come with an alternative recommendation, too.

—JOSEPH CRONIN
PRESIDENT AND CHIEF EXECUTIVE
OFFICER, SAATCHI & SAATCHI
DFS/PACIFIC

If I could turn back time, I would spend fewer hours working and more time with my children. They grew up without my constant contact and then moved away. Also, I never let my wife know what I did for a living and now I regret not sharing this part of my life. When you retire and want your spouse's help, it's very late.

I also wish someone had told me to make two or three very close friends and spend time with them. The ones I had were far away. I should have gone more often to see them and tell them how I feel instead of just doing this at funerals.

You will need people with whom you can talk out your problems. Many of mine would have been easier to handle by having my wife and best friends help me.

So my hindsight is to love your work, but also love your family and make a few friends, too. Participate in the lives of your growing children. You may not be as successful in your work, but you will be richer.

—Dr. Fred Kushner
Former Dean, Illinois College
of Optometry

Things Learned The Hard Way

Every good business will have its best years followed by lean years. Budget for the lean years.

After one or two years of success I see many businesses begin to believe that the good years will go on forever, and they begin to spend accordingly. They lease a new office, buy fancy furnishings, and hire excess employees to cover the peak workloads. Then when the lean years come, the new overhead becomes a killer.

—MIKE McCORMICK
PARTNER, LaRue, CORRIGAN &
McCORMICK

Always have the highest integrity, but also look out for yourself.

These two concepts can be synergistic. In turning around my company I was offered all of the stock. I took only half. I regret that decision to this day.

—JEFF HAINES
PRESIDENT AND CHIEF EXECUTIVE
OFFICER, ROYCE MEDICAL

Success is a matter of valuing things accurately at their true worth. Whether it concerns choosing the direction of your life, your company, your investments, or the companions who will accompany your journey, the ability to correctly assess reality is essential. We all get blinded by our emotions, our self-image, or our pride, and fail to see things as they really are. Being a very private person, I always chose to make independent and often unverified judgments.

On hindsight, it would have been helpful if someone told me that validation, or a "second opinion" from a trusted friend, could often help clarify my judgment. Nothing is as important as the accurate evaluation of our perceptions.

—BERT NEWMAN
CHIEF EXECUTIVE OFFICER,
THE NEWMAN CO., INC.

Many business mistakes are made when the economy is good and your company is doing well. People tend to relax when sales and profits are up. They tend to hire too many people and make investment decisions without the same thorough study that they would apply in difficult times. Several times I have seen large chemical companies expand at the top of the business cycle, only to suffer seriously when a recession follows.

—LARRY TUCKER
PRESIDENT, KT-PC, INC.

Things Learned The Hard Way

Nobody likes a smart-ass.

Twenty years ago I had an entry-level job as a brand assistant. My peers and I sat three to a cubicle. I used to entertain my wing of the building with imitations of some of our colleagues. None of the impressions were particularly flattering, but they did get laughs, and so I persisted.

Some years later I was interviewing for a job with another company. My prospective new boss thought it would be a good idea to meet the new client I would be working with—someone from those old days. At dinner he told me: "You know you really didn't make a lot of friends with your impressions of _____." A couple of sobering lessons from this:

1.   I had forgotten what I had done. *I* may have forgotten, but the people I hurt never would.

2.   It's never, *ever,* worth trying for a laugh at someone else's expense.

I was lucky. The new client and I made peace. But I remain excruciatingly aware of how easy it is to put a lasting tarnish on one's reputation. And no, I don't do wiseass humor anymore.

—BRUCE MILLER
PRESIDENT, SUISSA-MILLER
ADVERTISING, INC.

Things Learned The Hard Way

Say what you want to say when you have the feeling and the chance. Tomorrow can be one day too late.

Of all the things I have done, my deepest regrets are the things that I did not do, the opportunities missed and the things unsaid.

—CAPTAIN JIM KELLER
CHIEF PILOT, AMERICAN AIRLINES,
LOS ANGELES INTERNATIONAL
AIRPORT

Jim Keller manages more than one thousand pilots based at LAX for American Airlines. In 1991 he lost his only son, Chris, age fifteen, to a heart attack. Since then Jim has grieved privately while reaching out to help hundreds of other bereaved parents through The Compassionate Friends chapter he and his wife, Sandy, helped found. They committed their efforts to the memory of Chris.

Years ago I wish someone had told me to stop letting my hormones hog-tie my head.

I wish someone had told me not to put all my eggs of ambition into one basket marked "Marriage." A man will come along for you. . . . That's the easy part. What is hard is the same thing that is hard for everyone—excelling in the world in a field you choose.

Twenty-five years ago, young women got this garbled message: "Education is important but don't expect to really use it . . . except to provide a culturally stimulating home for your family." Professional achievement was barely on the radar screen as a female goal.

While much of that has changed, some still exists. I urge young women to be very clear about their dreams . . . to be more focused and less willing to compromise. I urge them to put love and marriage in perspective. To the daughter I never had I would say simply, "Performing well in work you love is the greatest high in the world."

Now as I collect my first Social Security check, I can't help but wonder on hindsight what I might have accomplished. Today's young woman should never have to wonder.

—Lyn Teven,
Freelance writer

THINGS YOU'LL DEFINITELY

FIGURE OUT EVENTUALLY
FOR YOURSELF BUT WHY
NOT HEAR THEM NOW
THUS SAVING YOURSELF
YEARS OF AGGRAVATION
AND HEARTACHE TO SAY
NOTHING OF TROUBLE
WITH A CAPITAL "T"

Things You'll Definitely Figure Out Eventually for Yourself But Why Not Hear Them Now Thus Saving Yourself Years of Aggravation and Heartache to Say Nothing of Trouble With a Capital "T"

Safe living generally makes for regrets later on.

We are all given talents and dreams. Sometimes the two don't match. But more often than not, we compromise both before ever finding out.

Later on, as successful as we might be, we find ourselves looking back longingly to that time when we should have chased our *true* dreams and our *true* talents for all they were worth.

Don't let yourself be pressured into thinking that your dreams or your talents aren't prudent. They were never meant to be prudent. They were meant to bring joy and fulfillment into your life.

People who love what they do are usually those people who are doing what they love.

—PETER SERCHUK
EXECUTIVE CREATIVE DIRECTOR,
MCCANN-ERICKSON/LOS ANGELES

Peter Serchuk is a creative and business leader during the day, and a gifted poet on his own time (*Waiting for Poppa at the Smithtown Diner, Poems by Peter Serchuk*). Every morning Peter wakes at 5:00 and goes into his den to write poetry. Then, at 7:30 he drives to the office and helps manage a $150 million business. He is a man who has clearly chased both his talent and his dreams.

D
on't be afraid or ashamed of believing in God, and of maturing spiritually.

—BILL BEAN
CHAIRMAN, STRATEGIA

Bill Bean lectures throughout the world on optimizing corporate performance. He also applies his unique strategic planning to individuals through a program called "Living on Purpose." The program identifies ten life categories that represent the dimensions of a well-rounded life: personal, health, recreation, family, friends, community, career, financial, household, and spiritual. Interestingly, Bill arranges these categories in a circle like pieces of a "life pie," but puts "spiritual" in the center, signifying its importance. These pieces or slices seem to be different sizes relative to each other at different times in our lives. But all are important.

Check yourself out regularly on each of the dimensions. If one piece of your pie is very large, and another is a tiny piece or not there at all, perhaps you should seek more balance.

We live life looking forwards but we understand it looking backward. As I look backward, what stands out is that things always come down to people. People *do* make a difference.

And the most important enduring aspect of a person's ability to make a difference comes not from brains or motivation, but from character. And at the heart of character is an old-fashioned value that is overlooked and underrated. Trust. Every human transaction rests, either explicitly or implicitly, on a foundation of trust . . . or lack thereof. Or so it seems to me.

Certainly not a new perspective. But, as I look back at my own life, these things seem more important than ever.

—NORMAN W. BROWN
RETIRED CHAIRMAN & CHIEF
EXECUTIVE OFFICER,
FOOTE, CONE & BELDING

Your boss's secretary can be one of your best career friends—or one of your worst enemies.

Nobody told me this. I had to work it out for myself. Too many people graduating with an MBA get so caught up with peers and bosses that they fail to appreciate the degree of influence that a good secretary has on her boss. Being friendly, appreciative, and complimentary goes a long way in developing an invaluable ally.

I passed this hindsight on to my own son as he began his business career, and he later told me that it was the single most useful advice he received.

—JOE E. DAVIS
INVESTMENT ADVISOR,
ENTREPRENEUR

Things
You'll
Definitely
Figure Out
Eventually
for Yourself
But Why
Not Hear
Them
Now Thus
Saving
Yourself
Years of
Aggravation
and
Heartache
to Say
Nothing of
Trouble
With a
Capital "T"

In finance, the smaller the type and the cheaper the paper it is printed on, the more important the information.

—INVESTOR'S RULE

Listening is the most difficult skill to learn, and the most important to have. In our business of advertising, learning how to listen—and really hear—what people are saying can make all the difference. When you listen well you hear:

✍ what consumers say and what they really mean

✍ what your clients are really looking to achieve, including hidden agendas

✍ what your people think is important about their jobs, their families, and their personal ambitions

Learning to talk is relatively easy. Spend twice as much time learning to listen as you do learning to talk.

—Lynn Upshaw
Chief operating officer,
Ketchum Advertising/
San Francisco

Even today when I go into a meeting I put a big "L" in the upper right hand corner of my note pad. It is a reminder to myself to "Listen first, dummy. Just shut up and listen." Sometimes I even visualize the person across the table from me sitting and swinging on that big "L."

Build in enough "fluff" to include unexpected changes in your business plan.

I know you have probably heard this before, but it is a common trap. When putting together projections for banking or venture capital, do not hesitate to inflate your estimated costs. Your legal and accounting bills will be double what you anticipate. And make your revenue projections very conservative. What you think will be there often is not. Then cut at least another 10 percent.

If you select one key individual when you start out, make it your controller. I thought I could get away with a lightweight, and I was wrong.

Finally, your most important asset is money itself. You will need

more than you expect. I was told
this and didn't believe it.

—MICHAEL DRAKE,
CHIEF EXECUTIVE OFFICER,
MIDA INDUSTRIES, INC.

Things You'll Definitely Figure Out Eventually for Yourself But Why Not Hear Them Now Thus Saving Yourself Years of Aggravation and Heartache to Say Nothing of Trouble With a Capital "T"

This summarizes tips for writing the perfect business memo:

1. For the rest of your life begin every memo with the word "This." It allows you to get started, and to tell the reader in the first sentence what the purpose of the memo is.

2. If it's under $3 million, put it on a single page. This forces you and your reader to focus only on what is really important. Additional information can be added as exhibits.

3. There are three reasons for everything. Never two or four. If you have two, make another one up. If you have four, cut one out.

—PROCTER & GAMBLE COMPANY
UNWRITTEN AND UNOFFICIAL
GUIDELINES

Go get international experience.

—PETER SEALEY
FORMER SENIOR VICE-PRESIDENT,
GLOBAL MARKETING,
THE COCA-COLA COMPANY

People born before 1965 are the last generation that can climb to the top of their company with work experience only in the United States. Those born from approximately 1965 on must go get international experience. That doesn't mean travel. It means living and working abroad. If you have an opportunity for an international assignment with your firm while you are in your twenties or early thirties, grab it, regardless of apparent impact on your domestic career. It will pay great dividends later.

Also become conversant in two foreign languages—one from Europe or South America—and one from Asia.

Working hard is very important, but remember to smell the flowers along the way. Doodle, dream, and always keep a sense of humor. And wear a bow tie.

It's easier to lean down to smell the flowers.

—MORGAN CHU
SENIOR PARTNER & MEMBER OF
EXECUTIVE COMMITTEE,
IRELL & MANELLA

In 1994 the *National Law Journal* named Morgan Chu one of the 100 most influential lawyers in the United States.

Twenty-five years ago I was busy learning to program a computer system that had no memory and no ability to store programs. In fact, it had less power than a five-dollar digital wristwatch. Today that technology is shaking every business and social relationship.

Looking ahead, the tools for greatness will continue to be knowledge of arts and letters. Without the ability to reason, no technology can help. But computer understanding and on-line fluency will be the twenty-first century's equivalent to basic reading skills. Without a thorough working knowledge, you will be a lost casualty of the information age.

—JOHN UPPGREN
CHIEF INFORMATION OFFICER,
GAGE MARKETING GROUP

Long before joining McCann-Erickson and becoming its chairman, Gene and his young partners founded the Norman, Craig and Kummel agency in New York. When they were just a tiny new agency, they lost their prized Revlon account, which was 40 percent of their entire business. But Gene rebounded the next day and had the nerve to make a cold new business call on the giant Colgate-Palmolive Company. The response was muffled laughter. The Colgate management asked, "Why in the world should we hire you, a thirty-year-old kid from a small agency just starting out?" Gene paused for a moment, and then answered "Because if you hire us, you will really be hiring five agencies. You see," Gene went on, "your other four agencies are very big but very asleep. If you hire us—young

Always, always be aggressive.

—GENE KUMMEL
CHAIRMAN EMERITUS,
McCANN-ERICKSON WORLDWIDE

Things You'll
initely Figure
Eventually fo
Yourself But
Not Hear The
Now Thus Sa
Yourself Year
Aggravation a
Heartache to
Nothing of Tr
ble With a Ca
"T"

and hungry and aggressive—you will shock the industry and suddenly wake up your other four agencies. And by doing that, you will get better advertising from each of them."

Gene got the business. Years later Norman, Craig and Kummel was not only a major agency in its own right, but had become the largest agency working worldwide for Colgate-Palmolive.

THINGS LEARNED ALONG THE WAY

Things
Learned
Along
The Way

Take time to sharpen the saw.

—CHARLES "RED" SCOTT
RETIRED PRESIDENT AND CHIEF
EXECUTIVE OFFICER,
ACTIVA GROUP

Red tells the story of a young man walking through a forest. He came upon an older man busily sawing a giant tree with a rusty saw. He watched the man get nowhere for a while and then went on his way. On his return trip, he again passed the old man still sawing away at the same tree. Finally, he shouted, "Hey, old man, you aren't getting anywhere. You need to stop and sharpen the saw." The old man looked up, sweat pouring from his cheeks, and yelled back, "Ain't got time, son, ain't got time."

We all need to take time to stop and sharpen our saw, not just hack away at the world. This might mean taking a seminar, reading a book, learning a new field, or just spending quiet time thinking. Don't just work hard; work smart.

Pick the best people you can to work for you, and trust them so that they can do their very best work for you and for themselves.

—MYRNA BLYTH
PUBLISHING DIRECTOR AND EDITOR
IN CHIEF, <u>LADIES' HOME JOURNAL</u>

Customers and clients are what give you power and independence. What matters is the business you control, not just how good you are.

When I joined the law firm where I was to remain for twenty-five years, the managing partner said to me: "Len, don't worry about getting business, just service the hell out of our clients, and all will be well. We'll worry about getting new clients. You worry about keeping them."

I followed that advice for too long. When I became a young partner, I continued to "service the hell out of clients" and, as a result, I built some fine long-lasting friendships. But I didn't seek business—business that I could call mine and that my partners would recognize as "mine." I mouthed all the platitudes about "firm client," not "my client" or "your client." And while I did this, others in my firm continued to attract and claim clients.

Then one day I realized that the rules had changed. What determined your power was the business you controlled, not just how good a lawyer you were. Pretty stupid for a so-called smart guy.

I write this without regrets. But, I tell young lawyers, always become the best lawyer you can be, but *never, never* forget to seek business whenever and wherever you can.

—LEONARD ORKIN
PARTNER, WINSTON &
STRAWN/NEW YORK

Hire slowly. Fire quickly. It's not the people you fire that hurt you. It's the people you don't fire.

—MARCIO MOREIRA
VICE CHAIRMAN, MANAGER—
ASIA AND PACIFIC
McCANN-ERICKSON WORLDWIDE

Things
Learned
Along
The Way

There are three virtues I have come to appreciate after twenty-five years.

The first is integrity. Be honest and straightforward in your communications and demand the same from people you deal with. Otherwise, any relationship is doomed.

The second is the art of persuasion. You cannot successfully command or demand, only persuade. Except for the simplest tasks, people must be motivated.

The third is simplicity. A simple, elegant solution can be understood, developed, and implemented. With each complicating factor, the probability of success diminishes exponentially.

—DANIEL T. SCOTT
CHAIRMAN AND CHIEF
EXECUTIVE OFFICER,
SCOTT PRINTING CORPORATION

1. Unconventional hair, beards, tattoos, earrings, and clothing will cost you more than a million dollars in lost income over the course of your business career. If you want to play the part, look the part.

2. Trust your gut. Business administrators rely upon facts and figures, and suppress intuition. Don't! Every time, without exception, when I have dealt with an individual who seemed to have a promising deal, but who otherwise made my skin crawl a bit, either business or personal problems have followed. Trust your subconscious feelings. They result from a lifetime of experience.

—RUSS HANLIN
PRESIDENT AND CHIEF EXECUTIVE
OFFICER, SUNKIST GROWERS, INC.

Do three things a year that will make a difference in your business. Know what they are and stick with them.

—Tom Laco
FORMER EXECUTIVE VICE-
PRESIDENT, PROCTER & GAMBLE
COMPANY

Procter & Gamble used to have what it called "budget meetings." These were annual inquisitions before top management to "defend" the recommended budget for next year. Many management questions were very detailed.

Tom was different. He would lean back in his chair after everybody else was done, and always ask this same question: "What are the three things, young man, that you will accomplish next year that will make a meaningful difference?" Tom's feeling was that the most you could really do to change a business were three things. The rest was housekeeping. The key was to decide what they were, and focus on them.

Life isn't fair. It isn't going to be fair. Stop sniveling and whining and go out and make it happen for you.

In business I see too many people who expect the financial tooth fairy to come at night and remove that ugly dead tooth from under the pillow and substitute profitability just in the nick of time at the end of their fiscal year.

—Dick Butler
Advertising Executive and
International Consultant

Never have a closed mind. Be inquisitive about everything. Study. Ask questions. Be curious. Always be open to learn. Follow up on things—you can never tell where they will lead.

Years ago I was quoted in the press about a campaign my agency had done for a client. An acquaintance wrote a letter to the editor challenging my comment. I wondered why that person felt the way he did, so I simply called him and asked. That phone call turned into a conversation. That conversation turned into a meeting. That meeting turned into a relationship, and that relationship turned into my joining Doyle Dane Bernbach as president of their San Francisco office.

All because I just wondered . . . .

—JERRY GIBBONS
SENIOR VICE-PRESIDENT, WESTERN
REGION—AMERICAN ASSOCIATION
OF ADVERTISING AGENCIES

Things
Learned
Along
The Way

Perhaps the one thing I wish I had been told years ago was to be prepared. As simple as this advice is, I'm constantly amazed at how ill-prepared people are.

Try to never go into a business meeting without knowing or at least thinking about what the outcome might be. In advance of the meeting prepare reactions to what you believe will be other people's agendas, and note the points you wish to make. In making films— and in life—the most important part of the process is preparation. I feel that every dollar spent wisely in preparation saves five in production and post-production.

—DENNIS BROWN
FORMER EXECUTIVE VICE-
PRESIDENT, NBC PRODUCTION

You are only able to go as far as your self-esteem will let you.

We all limit ourselves. Our own self-image, learned through example or experience, stops us. It's sort of a self-fulfilling prophecy. If we don't think we can, we won't.

They don't teach self-esteem in school. You alone are in charge of recognizing and accepting your attitude about yourself.

—BERNARD CHAISSON
REGIONAL SALES MANAGER,
AMERICAN HONDA

Don't let yourself "fogey up."

If it happened more than five years ago, forget it. It's irrelevant to what's going on today. Unlike many other businesses, film marketing is a business of the moment. Consumers change. Trends change. So five years ago is ancient history. Keep current. Past experience alone is never enough.

—BUFFY SHUTT
PRESIDENT OF MARKETING,
UNIVERSAL PICTURES

I wish someone had told me that age and experience aren't necessarily the recipe for competence. Too many times early in my business career I observed more mature people and assumed that, because of their age and position, excellence was guaranteed.

When I completed graduate school I joined a midsized New York Stock Exchange company as a mergers and acquisitions analyst. The company divided its operations into five groups with five group vice-presidents. These senior people had little familiarity with the products or services we rendered and no idea what they were managing.

—J. TERRANCE LANNI
PRESIDENT AND CHIEF EXECUTIVE
OFFICER, MGM GRAND, INC.

Hire outstanding people.

It is not only the difference between good results and great results. It adds "fun." When you work with outstanding people, everyone adds topspin to the business effort, and the team members work well together. Before I joined Arby's, I was President of El Pollo Loco restaurants in Southern California. I put together a really small team, but made up of really good people. In less than a year the business was repositioned, growing rapidly, and making money. We worked hard, but we had a ball!

—DON PIERCE
PRESIDENT AND CHIEF EXECUTIVE
OFFICER, ARBY'S INC.

Forget about it. It's yesterday's rain.

When I was working on the Interpublic acquisition of the Bates agency and we were finally outbid by Saatchi, for a while I kept musing if I had done this or that differently, maybe we could have made that transaction. But it turned out for the best.

I can remember being disappointed that I wasn't chosen to be Chief Financial Officer for a regional job for a Fortune 500 company, and it bothered me for almost a year. But I got on with it, and over the years ended up being CFO for three Fortune 500 corporations.

—Eugene P. Beard
Executive Vice-President,
Finance and Operations,
The Interpublic Group of
Companies, Inc.

Vision, determination, and hard work are not always enough. Failure sometimes means simply that others do not share your dreams.

Commit yourself to work that contributes to the social good— and commit yourself with equal energy to the society closest to home, your family.

Education is a lifetime pursuit. Success requires the constant acquisition of knowledge and skills to compete in a world of accelerated change.

—CHARLES E. YOUNG
CHANCELLOR, UCLA

Don't sail between the whales.

We all meet a lot of "whales" in our lives, and I have always found that it is better not to sail between them.

One group of whales is your spouse and his or her parents. Never ever criticize your spouse's parents, or agree with your spouse when he does. Another group to avoid is two "bosses" at the same time. And finally, stay out of disagreements between two children, two students, or two employees. Let people work out their differences without your help. This will strengthen their relationships with each other, and avoid getting you squashed between the whales.

—DR. JANE H. LEUTHOLD
PROFESSOR OF ECONOMICS,
UNIVERSITY OF ILLINOIS

Twenty-five years ago I wish someone had told me that I could "do it all," but probably not *all* at the same time or *all* by myself.

In my forties, I had teenagers at home, a national book tour, a consulting business, a house to remodel, and my husband in a career crisis. I ended up in the hospital.

It was then I began to learn the value of friendships, letting go of control, and asking someone else for help. I added a quality to my life that included fun, laughter, balance, and close friendships. Taking myself, my business, and my success so seriously wasn't working.

—SANDRA WINSTON
AUTHOR OF THE ENTREPRENEURIAL
WOMAN

To find stars, ask stars.

As an executive recruiter I am paid by my client company to find and recruit candidates who are real stars. What I have discovered is that the best way to locate these people is to ask other top "stars" for their recommendations. Average performers will tend to recommend other people like themselves. Stars will recommend stars.

—CHARLES HARREUS
FOUNDER, HARREUS & ASSOCIATES

Don't be afraid to be different from those around you. There is no one answer. I was too concerned about "fitting in" at General Foods. What the company really needed was people who would just do what it takes to get the job done.

—TOM ROMIG
FORMER PRESIDENT, MATTEL TOYS,
SPORTS DIVISION

Things
Learned
Along
The Way

You don't own any part of a small company's privately held Founder's Stock if you own less than 51 percent. Control is like winning. It's not one thing. It's everything.

—ERIC STROMSBORG
PRESIDENT, KETT ENGINEERING

Things
Learned
Along
The Way

Adages for Ad Agencies

1. The ultimate client is the Consumer, lose her and all is lost.

2. All problems are "creative" problems sooner or later.

3. Put your trust in simple ideas, simple sentences, and simple arithmetic.

4. Mistrust four-syllable words and continued reports of tranquility.

5. Beware of management by total surprise.

6. Large meetings are often used to share the blame.

7. It's easy to get a unanimous vote for doing nothing.

8. It is possible to make excellent television commercials within 100 miles of home.

9. Most people put a low value on what they do not know how to do themselves.

10. It is difficult to build a backlog of good will; ill will, yes— but good will starts from scratch at 9:00 every morning.

—Paul Foley
Former Chairman of the
Board, The Interpublic Group
of Companies, Inc.

What happens to you in life is less a result of predictable consequences of decision and training, and more a result of a series of occurrences and our responses to them. These responses are shaped by our values, belief systems, and experiences more than formal education. Therefore we must learn from every encounter, and not just from those who carry the title "teacher."

Conversations with thousands of patients have taught me to (1) be flexible and create more than one image of life which can make you happy; (2) never equate yourself or your worth with your occupation; and (3) love people more than things.

—Dr. Lee Reitler
President, South Bay Medical
Group

Never follow a John Wooden.

John Wooden was the most successful coach in the history of college sports. He won ten NCAA Basketball Championships for UCLA in twelve years, seven of them in succession. His teams set the record for eighty-eight consecutive wins, and he became a legend.

When John retired at the peak of his career, he left a highly successful program for his coaching successor to inherit. However, one coach after another eventually followed John Wooden, but no successive coach was ever regarded as truly successful. Winning wasn't good enough. The normal measures of evaluating performance had been stretched beyond human capabilities. After John Wooden, no achievement less than *perfect* could be good enough.

Occasionally, a similar circumstance can occur in business. A highly successful business led by a "legend" needs a new leader. Now assume you are recruited for the job. Stay away! Stop! Run, baby, run!

This kind of situation is not healthy for your career. These kinds of opportunities can only lead to unrealistic expectations, little credit for a job well done, and absolutely no fun on the job.

Never follow a John Wooden. Instead, accept a challenge where there's upside room to grow. Then you can *be* a John Wooden, not follow one.

—JIM HELIN
FORMER MANAGING DIRECTOR,
DMB&B/LOS ANGELES

Good people come in lots of different packages.

I admire those who have been able to deal with people from every walk of life. Malcolm Forbes was an example to me. At his funeral there were ex-presidents and bikers from the Hell's Angels—both calling him friend.

Celebrate diversity and use it to your advantage. In business 95 percent of the intelligence in an organization is often several layers below "management." The shipping clerk can tell you to how to fix a problem. Your secretary knows what's really going on. The receptionist hears what customers really think of your firm. If you would only ask. It's okay to talk to strangers.

—Bill Flatley
Director of Advertising,
Forbes Magazine

Twenty-five years ago I wish someone had told me that the enduring meaning in my life would be found in shaping my children's values, not in my professional success.

I have also learned that people go through phases. What seems obvious and absolute at age twenty or thirty may be viewed more skeptically later in life.

—RABBI HAROLD S. KUSHNER
AUTHOR & RABBI LAUREATE,
TEMPLE ISRAEL, NATICK, MASS.

Chill out.

—EVERYBODY

Almost everybody who responded to the question, "What do you wish someone had told you twenty-five years ago?" provided this addendum to their hindsight in one form or another.

Of course, we all need to work hard, focus on our goals, and try to balance the key segments of our lives. But we also need to relax, enjoy each day, take 100 percent responsibility for our own happiness, and pick more daisies.

Remember that the chance of a sperm and egg uniting is 200 million to one. Each of us has already won the biggest lottery grand prize of all—we are here to read this book.

Chill out and relax. This thing called life is a great place to be.

AND FINALLY:

THE AUTHOR'S VERY OWN
AND PARTICULAR
HINDSIGHTS

And Finally:
The Author's
Very Own
Particular
Hindsights

For several years I have researched other people's answers to the question "What do you wish someone told you twenty-five years ago?" Here are my own:

1. *Follow your dream.*

Become the person you really are inside. Listen to that "still small voice" that was the person you were as a teenager. That is the real you. Don't necessarily do what others think you should do. Do what you love with all your heart, and everything else, usually including money, will follow.

To follow your dreams, simply turn them into goals, what Marjorie Blanchard calls "dreams with deadlines." Write your goals down but don't share them with anyone. That way you will be totally honest with yourself. Carry them with you and refer to them often. You will find that the whole world seems to part way for someone who has a sense of where he is going.

2. *Hug your family.*

Your family is more important than you think, and will be gone sooner than you expect. I have three pictures on my desk. One is of me with my parents. The other two are with my wife and sons on family vacations. I don't have any pictures of me at the office, working late, making the "deal," or going to black-tie dinners. I don't have a picture of me making a deposit at a bank-teller window, flying first-class to Tokyo, or returning a 28 percent margin to my company. Just the family.

Usually a child goes off to college or career at age seventeen. That's seventeen years out of an eighty-five-year lifetime that you will have your children at home—20 percent of your life.

In our family, my wife never missed a soccer game, swim meet, or volleyball game as the kids grew up. I don't mean she made most of the games—she attended every one—while still holding down a full-time career as a real estate broker. I was off doing "important stuff" at the office, while she was there for the boys every day. I love her for that.

3. *Find a faith that works for you.*

Faith is, for most of us, a very personal thing. You may not need your faith today or next year. It may be twenty years. But the time will come. Find a way to center yourself in the spiritual as well as the other areas of business, personal, and family life. Faith can't be proven, of course. But just trust your intuition. Alfred Lord Tennyson said, "Because of what I have seen, I trust in what I cannot see."

In closing, my wish for you is that you will enjoy each moment and not feel selfish about doing so. In Nadine Stair's words, "Eat more ice cream . . . ride more merry-go-rounds . . . pick more daisies." Celebrate this evening's sunset. Did you see it? Cherish the fellowship of truly good friends. When did you call them last? Take time to notice the woods you loved so much when you were a tree-climbing kid. Have you come to take them for granted? Be at peace with yourself about who you are.

Finally, relax and enjoy the ride. Yesterday is gone. Tomorrow isn't here. But today is absolutely glorious. And it is yours to enjoy.

Have a wonderful next twenty-five years.

CONTRIBUTORS

CONTRIBUTORS